Once Ransomed

Love in Christ,
Jane Shannon
Psalm 34:4

A TRUE STORY OF KIDNAPPING & REDEMPTION

Once Ransomed

DICK PARKER in collaboration with TANE SHANNON

Published by Looking Glass Books
730 Sycamore Street
Decatur, Georgia   30030
(404) 371-1236

Author's Note

Once Ransomed is based primarily on the experiences and recollections of Tane Shannon, with additional information drawn from court documents, FBI and sheriff's department records, and from interviews with investigators, witnesses, clergy, family members and friends. Donnie Ray Radford declined a request for an interview. Exact quotes, when used, come from documents or from recollections of participants in the conversations.

To my husband, Mike, whom I love with all my heart —
a man who loves me in spite of my faults and who is my very
best friend in the world. To my mom and dad for always being there when I needed them, for loving me when I was
unlovable, and for giving me wonderful childhood memories. To my brother for being so much more than just a brother.
To my grandparents for being such a big part of my life and
for being Godly role models throughout my childhood. And
to my cousin Sherri, who was always like my big sister. I love
you all and I thank God every day for bringing us together as
a family. But above all, this book is dedicated to God, who
loves me so much he allowed me to experience an incredibly
spiritual night, and He showed me how powerful prayer is
and how magnificent He truly is.

— Tane Shannon

Once
Ransomed

One

You meant evil against me, but God meant it for good.
— Genesis 50:20

Sunday, August 9, 1992

All day long the sulfur-flecked mobile home under the trees had stayed cool, but now the sun moved to the one spot in the white sky where leaves didn't block it. Like a tin can, the thing heated up fast. When he began to sweat, the man inside got up from the kitchen floor and turned on the window-unit air conditioner. He stood for a moment in the whirr, lifting his shirt to let the cold, dry air blow directly on him, then he returned to the brown linoleum and resumed his task.

Wearing latex surgical gloves, he picked up a red felt-tip pen with his right hand and put it between the first two toes of his right foot. He held a yellow legal pad steady with his gloved hands, then curled his toes around the pen and began to write.

When he rented the trailer from Bonnell Davis on Friday, he had told her, "I'm a grown man and I need to be out on my own." He was nearly forty years old and had lived with his parents since his release from prison. He didn't mention the prison part to Mrs. Davis.

Now that he was free, all he needed was money and a woman. Lots of money and one particular woman.

✝ ✝ ✝

Tane Robson Shannon chased her giggling three-year-old daughter through the maze of moving boxes on the living room floor.

"Gimme that duck!" Tane cried.

But Kaylan didn't stop. When Tane caught her, she grabbed the yellow rubber duck making it squeak, then she hugged Kaylan and tickled her, and they both laughed until they cried.

That's how the whole weekend went. With a three-year-old and a one-year-old in the house, packing to move to the Shannon's new home degenerated into a constant game of chase or hide-and-seek. The only time Tane and her husband, Mike, relaxed was when they went to church on Sunday morning. Even then, Tane made mental lists of things to be packed and hardly listened to the sermon, including the preacher's answer to what he called the world's greatest question: "What must I do to be saved?"

Tane had heard the answer a hundred, maybe a thousand times in her twenty-eight years — so many times that it seemed almost trite. Believe in the Lord Jesus and you will be saved. Believe in the Lord Jesus and you will be saved. She believed. She was saved. She did that a long time ago. Now, where could she put all those boxes piled up in the living room floor?

She knew Kaylan and Mick would be crying to leave the nursery, so Tane hardly listened to the closing prayer. Dr. John Lee Taylor prayed specifically for her, although not even he knew it. "I pray today, Father, that none of us will leave this room without the assurance that whatever life may bring, Jesus Christ will meet it with us. Not only would we live this life, but we would walk into the portals of Heaven knowing in Whom we have believed."

✝ ✝ ✝

The man's work dragged on. Using his feet to write was agonizingly slow, but he couldn't risk recognition. The inside of the trailer darkened as thunderheads boiled up on the horizon and dusk settled over the mountains. He had written four notes which lay on the floor in a circle around him, and his toes were beginning to cramp. Someone knocked at the thin aluminum front door. The man didn't move. The knock came again and the door squeaked open a few inches.

"Donnie?" It was Mrs. Davis. His car was parked out front, so there was no denying that he was inside. But she couldn't come in. Not now. He stayed still.

Another knock.

"Don? You in there?"

He was eight feet away, behind a partial wall. Without the noise from the air conditioner she might have heard him breathing. Two of his notes were visible from the door if she opened it all the way.

"Donnie?"

She opened the door a few more inches then closed it and left. He waited a minute before looking around the corner to be sure she had closed it all the way. The pillow she had promised to bring lay against the wall. He locked the door.

The crisis past, the man gathered his notes from the floor and tore open a box of freezer bags. Still wearing the gloves, he put one note in each bag and carefully zipped it shut. He found the strapping tape he had bought and reached into his pocket for his knife. He cut a piece of tape for each bag to reinforce the seals. Then he put on his socks and tennis shoes and drove off to deliver them.

TWO

No man can redeem the life of another or give to God a ransom for him.
— *Psalm 49:7*

Spring 1994

Jackie Beavers had reason to be skeptical. A longtime Sunday School teacher and Christian counselor, she had been told of experiences like Tane's before, of people who found religion in foxholes. Too often they returned to life-as-usual after the crisis — especially women like Tane, who had beauty, money, friends, a devoted husband and children — forgetting the commitments they had made and minimizing the salvation they had claimed.

More than a year after God's rescue, which followed a lifetime of backsliding, Tane was still proving to herself that she wasn't going to forget this time. She was afraid to forget. She had read Hebrews 6:4-6, and the words scared her. "It is impossible for those who have once been enlightened ... if they fall away, to be brought back to repentance, because to their loss they are crucifying the Son of God all over again and subjecting Him to public disgrace."

"God got me out of that trailer alive," Tane told Jackie as they sat at Jackie's kitchen table. "Really. And He showed me that night what Heaven was like. I saw it right there. So I can't ever be like I was again. I just can't be. What would He do?"

Jackie didn't answer immediately and Tane shifted uncomfortably in the silence. Finally, Jackie said, "First of all, I think God got you away from that man for a reason. I don't know what it is, and you probably don't either, but you didn't earn your escape. You just have to accept it as grace.

"The other question, about whether you'll fall back into your old ways, you'd better know what you're up against because every life is a battle between the powers of darkness and light. That's the fight you fought and lost so many times before. And you'll keep fighting it even now that you've seen God's goodness. We can't begin to know or comprehend all of the systems involved, but when you read your Bible you'll see the influence of evil spirits all over the place. You can see it in your own life.

"When you were growing up, Satan appeared to you as an angel of light. He made the evil choices appear desirable: sex, alcohol, wild parties. He had to do it that way because if he came with a pitchfork and a tail, you'd turn away every time. And at some point, with his guile, Satan kidnapped you from your highest and best."

Tane had never considered before then that she had been kidnapped twice, but it made sense.

"And let me tell you something else," Jackie added. "When he got you, no amount of your daddy's or Mike's money could have set you free. The Psalmist wrote, 'No man can redeem the life of another or give to God a ransom for him.' Only you could make the decision and only Christ could pay the ransom."

Three

"I baptize you with water for repentance."
— *Matthew 3:11*

September 1973

Throughout the service nine-year-old Tane had sat with her mother and father and brother about middle of the way back, staring at the empty baptismal pool behind the choir and wondering if she was tall enough to touch bottom when it was full. She was smaller than most of her fourth-grade friends. She couldn't tell how deep it was because of the partial wall in front of it.

She hadn't told anybody she was going to do it. In fact, she wasn't sure herself until she heard Rev. Boswell say before the closing hymn, "I invite anyone to come to the altar in repentance and faith and confess their sins to Jesus Christ." Then they all stood and sang "I Am Thine, O Lord."

Tane thought the pool looked like a picture of the Jordan River in the Bible her mother had given her when she was six. A painting on the wall behind the pool showed trees and rocks and a waterfall spilling into a lake, which became real water when the pool was full. In the sky above the waterfall sun rays spewed from behind clouds like God does sometimes.

The painting was as big as life, and Rev. Boswell became a part of it, like John the Baptist in Tane's Bible, when the pool was full and he baptized people. Waves rose and fell against a glass panel at the top of the partial wall so the congregation could see the water. Tane was ready to be part of the picture.

As they sang the hymn, her mother held the book low enough for her to read the words. "Draw me nearer, nearer, blessed Lord, to the cross where Thou hast died ..."

In the weeks leading up to that Sunday, Tane had felt herself being drawn nearer. She read a few verses in her Bible almost every night and tried to understand them. What did it mean to be saved? Why did Jesus say, "The Son of Man gives His life as a ransom for many"? In Sunday School they had talked about Heaven and hell, and the teacher explained that anybody who was saved would go to Heaven. That's what Tane wanted. She was ready to commit herself. But why did she have to do it in front of everybody?

"That first step is hard," her teacher said. "But once you take it, the rest is easy."

Tane wasn't sure what she meant by that, but she knew that walking down the aisle would be hard. For four straight Sundays she thought she would do it. At home she had imagined everybody watching, especially Rev. Boswell, smiling, encouraging her to join the fold. Every Sunday, however, she got scared, and the final hymn ended before she moved her feet.

They started singing the second verse, "Consecrate me now to Thy service, Lord ..." but Tane didn't sing. She took her hand off the hymnal, looked up and saw only the backs of people standing in front of her. No faces. Not even the preacher. Her stomach knotted up and she leaned on the pew in front of her. She started sliding out, and her daddy and brother, who probably thought she was just going to the bathroom, stepped back so she could get around. And she still might have gone to the bathroom — turned left at the aisle instead of right. But when she reached the end of the pew, she looked right and there stood Rev. Boswell, all alone at the front, singing. She turned toward him and he smiled.

It wasn't at all like she had imagined it would be. His was the only face she saw. She walked in a straight line toward his singing smile, without looking to either side along the way. If she had turned from the smile, she might have run out the door. Who was watching her from behind? Were they smiling? What would her parents say? She couldn't look back. She hadn't told them she was even thinking about doing this. They might think she was weird.

She reached the front of the church and the preacher put his hand on her shoulder and leaned down. "Why, hello, Tane," he said while the congregation continued singing. "What has led you to the altar?"

"I want to be saved."

She thought he would be surprised, but he said without hesitation, "Oh, that's marvelous, just marvelous. Now I know you've talked about it in Sunday School, but are you sure you understand the meaning of what you're doing — what it means to give your life over to Jesus?"

"Yes, sir."

But she didn't understand the reciprocal and permanent nature of her covenant, and would not understand until God made it clear nearly twenty years later.

"Come right over here and let's sit together," Rev. Boswell said.

Tane and the preacher sat on the first pew.

Then Rev. Boswell looked directly at her and said, "Tane, if you confess with your mouth Jesus as Lord and believe in your heart that God raised Him from the dead, you shall be saved; for with the heart man believes, resulting in righteousness, and with the mouth he confesses, resulting in salvation. Do you confess Jesus as your Lord and Savior?"

"Yes sir," she said.

Then, still looking at her, he said, "For God so loved Tane that He gave His only begotten Son that whosoever believes in him should not perish but have eternal life."

Tane was warm and the back of her neck tingled. Then Rev. Boswell prayed softly, thanking God for bringing Tane to this important point in her life. She didn't hear all he said because she was still thinking about her parents. They must be wondering what she's doing up here — what they were talking about. The hymn ended and she and the preacher stood up.

"I'm delighted to tell you that Tane Robson has accepted Jesus Christ as her Lord and Savior," he said. "Milton and

Brenda and Todd, would you all come down here so the congregation can greet all of you?"

Tane's parents smiled broadly as they walked down the aisle, but Tane could see the question in their eyes. Why didn't you tell us? They hugged her when they reached the front. Then, row by row, everyone in Poplar Springs Baptist Church filed by and shook Tane's hand or hugged her and welcomed her into the family of Christ.

✟ ✟ ✟

On Sunday night Tane picked up her Bible and vowed to read it from cover to cover, Genesis to Revelation. She got from "In the beginning" to the seventh day, when God had completed his work and rested, before she was too sleepy to go on. She would start there tomorrow. Before she fell asleep she told God she would do what her Sunday School teacher said to do, bring others to Him.

On Monday morning she carried her Bible to school and told her fourth-grade class what she had done. A nine-year-old evangelist, she enlisted Rodney Sexton to help her save souls. Their first two marks were Ronnie Turk and Scott Cook, who could be a little smart alecky. Tane and Rodney cornered their prey during library time and made them sit quietly while they read verses to them. Then they made their converts-to-be recite the verses back.

Three weeks later Tane would take her second step as a new Christian: immersion. She read her Bible at night in preparation, and told everybody at school what she was learning. She called her grandmother, Mama Dese, to make sure she could come to her baptism, and she invited her basketball coach as well. Her mother made her a new yellow dress, sheer with white lining, that she would wear the day she would be baptized. "You won't actually go in the water with it," her mother explained. "You'll wear shorts for that."

When the day came, Rev. Boswell met Tane in his office behind the sanctuary for last-minute instructions as the Sunday morning service began. She wore no shoes, just socks, shorts and a blouse. He was in a black suit — his regular clothes. He prayed briefly then explained, "Now wait until I motion for you to come into the water, and when I say 'Holy Ghost,' you take a real deep breath and hold it."

They stood and walked to the doors that led to the baptismal font.

"Now I'll go down this side and you go down the other," he said.

Two hallway doors opened to stairways down to opposite sides of the font. Tane had to pull hard to open her door, then she stepped into a stairway that was so narrow she wondered how a full-grown person could fit in it. The door closed behind her. Down the steep carpeted stairs she went, slowly, silently, both hands on the walls, all alone. At the turn halfway down, Tane could see the bottom step, light blue metal covered with still water. It would be cold. She hated stepping into a cold pool one step at a time. She would rather dive in all at once and get it over with.

At the bottom she would have to turn left to enter the pool. She stopped at the last dry step and looked around the corner. The water didn't look too deep. Rev. Boswell hadn't come down on his side yet so she sat down and took off her socks, then stuck one toe into the water to see how cold it was. It wasn't cold at all. It was like bath water. Relieved, she put both feet in, making little waves that she could watch when she leaned forward. She listened for the preacher.

After a minute she heard a slork, slork sound and looked around the corner. Here came Rev. Boswell down the steps and into the water, wearing his robe and some rubber galoshes over his shoes. Tane figured they must be more like fishing waders because he took two more steps and the water was up to his waist, waves slapping against the painting and her feet.

He quoted some scripture and prayed and then motioned for Tane to join him. She stepped into the water until it came up so high it wet her long hair. But she was standing just fine.

Then she looked out toward the congregation, all of them watching her. The preacher looked out too, but his words focused on Tane, his slow, deep voice echoing within the walls of the font. He asked her some questions and she answered, "I do," and, "I will," then he said her sins and her old ways were dead, buried in a watery grave. She would walk in newness of life, in the death and resurrection of our Lord.

Tane concentrated on his every word, waiting for her cue. Then he said, "Dana Tane Robson, I baptize thee in the name of the Father, the Son and the Holy Ghost."

That was it. She took a deep breath and held it as he placed one arm and hand gently behind her back and head, and the other hand lightly over her face. He dipped her slowly backward so that she could see where the painting met the white ceiling high above her. Then, as her ears went under and the room went silent, she closed her eyes and breathed out through her nose, making bubbles to keep water out. Her small body relaxed in the warmth, supported by the preacher's arm and the water, which almost lifted her feet off the floor. She wanted to stay there, to float in the quiet darkness, to see Jesus walking toward her in the river. But as she exhaled she could feel herself getting heavier on the preacher's arm. He lifted her shoulders and head so that she was standing again, her wet hair heavy against her back. She opened her eyes and he was there beside her, and all the people in the pews were still looking at her. The preacher echoed another prayer and with his amen he turned toward the steps to leave. Tane assumed that meant she was supposed to leave too, so she went the opposite direction, to the stairs she had come down. She stepped out of the water clean and pure, dripping and soaking the carpet on the narrow stairs as she rose. She picked up her socks with two fingers and held them out to keep them dry.

Four

*They had breastplates like breastplates of iron, and the
sound of their wings was like the thundering of many horses
and chariots rushing into battle.*
— *Revelation 9:9*

Summer 1976

When she was a child, Tane thought Sunday was the
best morning of the week. She and her older brother, Todd,
often spent Saturday nights with their grandparents, Mama
Dese and Daddy Cliff. Their cousin Sherri lived there all the
time; she and her stepfather didn't get along. On weekends
Sherri, Todd and Tane indulged themselves in the spoils of
grandchildhood, playing Rook and watching TV. When they
went to bed, Tane and Sherri and Mama Dese all slept in the
king-size bed with Tane in the middle. Todd and Daddy Cliff
slept in the double bed in the next room, and Todd listened
jealously while the girls talked and laughed after the lights
went out.

On Sunday morning all the children drank coffee —
mostly milk and sugar. They went to church after breakfast,
Sherri, Todd and Tane giggling all the way in the back seat,
and sometimes Mama Dese told them Bible stories or about
God and how much He loved them.

Tane was eleven when Mama Dese let her shave her legs
one Saturday night, even though they both knew Tane's
mother had forbidden it. That afternoon Daddy Cliff had let
Tane and Todd take turns sitting in his lap while driving the
car through the big cemetery behind the house. Slowly around
the big circle Tane drove, stretching her arms wide to hold
the big steering wheel and craning to see over the dashboard.

Next, Sherri, who had just turned sixteen, practiced driving by herself. When she finished, she parked the car near
the big marble Bible, and they walked, Tane, Todd, Sherri
and their grandfather, to a brass plaque marking the grave of

Dorsey E. Whitmire, 1938-1960. Sherri knew her father only by pictures and this marker. He had been killed, shot dead, just a few miles away when she was a year old. The small group stood close and read the brass plate, which they all knew by heart, their four shadows falling across the grass. After a moment Daddy Cliff turned silently from his son's grave. The grandchildren followed slowly up a long sidewalk to the highest point in the cemetery, where a square marble building as high as a church gave Tane the creeps. The walls were lined with big drawers, and inside the drawers were dead people identified by brass plates. Tane wondered, but not for long, if they were in head first or feet first, then hurried to the other side, ready to run.

The wind almost always blew at the top of the hill. From there the quartet surveyed the entire cemetery, rolling, treeless, without a single raised headstone — perfect for sledding if it snowed deep enough. Every grave was marked with an identical brass plaque flat on the ground. Without another vertical distraction, the marble Jesus talking with the woman at the well halfway down the hill commanded that the eye come to Him. The grandchildren, in fact, ran to Him, twisting and turning and weaving to avoid stepping on a grave. They jumped up each of the five steps until the life-size Jesus towered over them. When Daddy Cliff arrived, he lifted Tane, who laughed all the way, over and into the four-foot-deep well. Her feet hit the discarded plastic flowers at the bottom, and she could barely see over the sides. Todd went in next, and the two of them ducked and hid in the well.

"Dinnertime," Daddy Cliff said to Sherri, and he started down the steps. "Let's go home."

Tane and Todd screamed in mock terror, certain their grandfather would come back for them, and relieved when he did. He lifted them out and they walked back to the car, stopping at the marble Bible where Daddy Cliff read the Lord's Prayer out loud.

Mama Dese stayed home and cooked supper while the

others played. She went to the cemetery often, but not so much with the grandchildren. Standing over Dorsey's grave was hard enough alone. The memory of that terrible, wonderful Monday night sometimes overwhelmed her.

Cliff was working late at the hatchery when Dese answered the phone just before midnight. Dorsey had gone from his own hatchery to Winston Allen's store for some cigarettes. He and Allen, who had a reputation for meanness and an arrest record to back it up, had argued. Shots had fired. Dorsey didn't have a gun. He was hurt bad. Dese and Cliff should come. Cliff's hatchery didn't have a phone, so Dese called her brother Robert, who sent his wife to find Cliff while he took Dese to Dorsey. Dese ran to her brother's car when he drove up. They turned out on Browns Bridge Road and were at the store in two minutes, before the ambulance arrived. Robert's headlights spotted Dorsey facedown in front of the store. He turned the lights away as Dese ran to him saying, "Please, God, don't let it be so! Not my boy!"

She didn't see the blood in the dark. A shotgun blast, the gun shoved in Dorsey's back, had killed him before he hit the ground. She knew he was gone. She knew it when she lifted his shoulders and when she put him down. The blood was on her hands, her clothes.

Two ambulances came with their flashing red lights and headlights that illuminated the damage from the shotgun. Cliff arrived and Dese ran to him. The sheriff drove up and Cliff told him he wanted to swear out a murder warrant against Allen, who said the whole thing was a mistake — the gun had gone off accidentally. One ambulance took Dorsey to the hospital. Another took Dese home. Cliff went to the hospital in his car, then came home. He would see the sheriff on Tuesday morning. It was all they could do.

Sometime after midnight Dese's brothers and sisters gathered at the house. While everybody sat or shuffled about in stunned silence, Dese lay on her bed, her wet eyes shut, praying hard. There was a Heaven and a hell, and Dorsey was in one or the other. Dese couldn't bear the thought of her own son suffering eternal damnation.

Her silent prayer carried her into a state between sleep and wake. Hers was a prayer of few words. God knew what she wanted, a sign that Dorsey was in Heaven. She believed he was. He had said he accepted Christ and he had been baptized. But the way he died, in an argument, shot down, she wondered. She prayed and waited and prayed again, and when she had prayed all she could, she rested. Her neck and shoulders relaxed and she let her hands fall onto the bed.

The overhead light came on, filtering through her eyelids, although she didn't hear the switch. She cracked her eyes to see. The light was not on after all, but the ceiling around the light was bright and growing brighter. She opened her eyes wide and her hands began to shake as she brought them to her face. White light, full of color and warmth, spread across the ceiling and downward, illuminating the entire room. Cliff stepped into the room, into the light, and walked toward her, saying something she could not hear. Her sorrow was lifted. She felt only joy that she could neither explain nor understand. Her whole body trembled and she heard herself laughing. This was her sign. Dorsey was all right. He was in Heaven. And if God's hand had reached out to her from the light, she would have reached back and gone to Him right then and there. At that moment she was ready to be with Him and Dorsey. Cliff leaned toward her and her sister came through the door. They mistook her laughter for delirium.

"I'm not crazy!" Dese cried, still laughing as she sat up. "I've got something to laugh about. Dorsey's okay. I know it."

The light went away when she spoke. She stood up and repeated, "Dorsey's okay. I know it now."

Startled by Dese's strange enthusiasm, other mourners came into the bedroom as Dese sang out the words again and again. Her euphoria continued even as she longed for the light, which she never expected to see again in this lifetime, to fill the room again.

✝ ✝ ✝

Charles Manson's eyes, wild and demonic, filled the television screen. Tane was twelve and she loved scary movies. Dese and Cliff stayed in the den reading while the kids watched TV in the living room. It was summer, so Tane, who was about to be a seventh grader, got to stay up late watching *Helter Skelter* at her grandparents' house with Sherri and her boyfriend, David. David's friend Brian, who was fifteen, watched with them. Sherri and David sat on the floor. Brian sat beside Tane on the sofa.

Everybody knew about *Helter Skelter* and Charles Manson and the gruesome murders his "family" committed in California. In 1969 Manson planned to make the Bible's book of Revelation a reality by starting a race war. He called himself Jesus Christ and said he would rule the world after Armageddon.

Tane barely noticed Brian's arm drape across the sofa above her shoulders as the camera focused on the blood and gore of five murders. His arm remained there as a member of the "family" described Manson's interpretation of Revelation 9. This part riveted Tane even more than the murders themselves. To Manson the four angels and the locusts in the passage represented the Beatles. Long hair, breastplates and scorpion's tails in verses eight, nine and ten were their hair, electric guitars and cords. Manson believed the Beatles spoke to him through their music and that the time for "helter skelter" was now. The Beatles' song Revolution 9 was the sound of the battle of Armageddon to Manson, who said he would become the fifth angel mentioned in verse one, the "king over them."

Tane made a mental note to read the ninth chapter of Revelation to see for herself.

A commercial interrupted the movie and Tane felt a light tug on her shoulder. She turned toward Brian and she knew what was coming, even though she had never kissed a boy on the mouth. He obviously hadn't been as interested in the movie. His eyes had that glazed-over look she had seen when people in movies kissed. She, like many twelve-year-olds, had practiced this moment often, kissing her arm or a pillow and wondering what it would feel like to really do it. She hadn't expected it tonight. She wasn't ready for it. She needed more practice. She wanted to do it first with a boyfriend, which she didn't have. In a couple of years, maybe. Brian's face moved slowly toward hers as his hand pulled her shoulders gently toward him. His eyes closed just as their lips touched. She closed her eyes next and felt him kiss her, long and wet. She was uneasy. He still held her gently, and she could have pulled away. She thought she wanted to pull away. She even told herself, "Pull away." But she didn't move. When he stopped kissing her, she watched and waited a moment for his eyes to open. They did not and he kissed her again. Finally he opened his eyes and smiled slightly. She smiled back automatically — she always smiled when somebody smiled at her.

The commercials ended and, without speaking a word, they turned back toward the television. Brian's arm held Tane tightly against him as they watched flashbacks of two more grisly murders committed on the weekend of August 9 and 10, 1969. The dates of those murders, insignificant to her at the time, immediately left Tane's memory. Later, August 10 would be seared into her mind. And in the intervening years, she would always associate her first kiss with *Helter Skelter*.

✜ ✜ ✜

David Bond told Tane about Rita Bell long before the two girls met. "She'll be your competition," David said. "Y'all will be the prettiest girls at South Hall." Tane wasn't looking for competition, but it would be neat to be one of the prettiest girls in junior high school.

David was right about Rita. Her long, straight hair was the color of honey, and her eyes seemed to catch the sun when she smiled, even when she was inside. Tane couldn't decide if Rita's clothes — a loose fitting skirt and jacket — were behind or ahead of the times, but they looked stylish on her and gave her an air of confidence. Her voice matched her whole look, soft and sweet.

Rita and Tane were perfect contrasts. Tane's hair was dark and wavy. She already was wearing tight jeans and tops that accentuated her developing figure, and when she spoke, everybody in the room heard her.

In one conversation the girls learned that they shared passions for roller-skating and country music while almost all of the other seventh graders were into rock 'n' roll. They quickly became best friends.

The second week of school Rita invited Tane to spend the night over on Friday. They would meet at Skate Country and Rita's mother would take them home. Tane was never more confident than when she was on the rink in her white skates with blue wheels, her hair blowing back from her face. She turned easily, skated backward and kicked up her feet during dance songs. Rita was good too, but she didn't have Tane's flash.

Rita shared a bedroom with her sister, Renee, so when they got home, Tane said she would sleep on the floor. Both Rita and Renee offered Tane their beds, but she really wanted to sleep on the floor. It would be like camping out. Rita thought that sounded fun, so she slept on the floor too.

Before they turned off the light, Rita read a few verses from her Bible on the bedside table.

"Do you read the Bible every night?" Tane asked.

"At least a little," Rita said.

Tane wished she read the Bible more. Maybe she could read just a few verses every night like Rita. Anybody could do that. She decided to start tomorrow.

But "tomorrow" would be a long time coming.

Five

Consider how the lilies grow.
– *Luke* 12:27

Monday, August 10, 1992
7:30 a.m.

The foot-scrawled notes left by the man wearing latex gloves were waiting for Mike Shannon when he drove to work on Monday morning. The man would have to give him instructions to find them. One was attached to the back of the Gainesville/Jefferson sign just north of Exit 6 on the interstate. Another was taped to the back of the county landfill sign on Athens Highway, and the third was taped to a sign that read, "Re-elect Bob Bates," in front of Jackson County High School, ten miles away in Jefferson. The man who wrote the notes would deliver the fourth one to the Shannons' home later that day.

Mike drove away from the rising sun toward his optometry office in Cumming, crossing the bridge over Lake Sidney Lanier as a lone fishing boat carved a V in the glassy water. On the horizon, the foothills of the Blue Ridge Mountains, more gray than blue, stretched and yawned, gathering the energy to rise nearly a mile into the sky by the time they reached the North Carolina border. Thinking through the business of his day, Mike rarely noticed the beauty of his early morning commute. After lunch he would drive ten more miles to his other office in Buford to see more patients. He hoped to be back home before Tane put the children to bed, but he didn't expect to be.

August left Mike little time to see anyone but patients. His appointment book overflowed with the names of children whose parents had waited until the end of summer to bring them in for eye examinations. Plus, the phone rang several times a day with emergencies, frequently patients who

19

had lost or broken their glasses while they were on vacation.

August 1992 was especially stressful. In addition to maintaining two optometry offices — three when he counted the laundry basket in his car filled with patient files and equipment — Mike and Tane were buying a new house, moving in a week, and they hadn't sold their existing one yet. Mike had loved their old house since the day they moved in. A creamy white Cape Cod on the north side of Gainesville, it sat against a backdrop of poplar and oak trees on a street with more bicycle than auto traffic. Now a "for sale" sign stood in the front yard beside Kaylan's blue plastic pool. The house was too far from Mike's offices. Moving south of town would eliminate an hour of driving time every day — time he could spend with his family. Or with additional patients. After six years he had established two steady, small-town practices. They generated the money his family needed, but he sometimes wondered at what cost.

Every morning he showered, shaved, dressed and went downstairs where Tane, laughing with Kaylan and Mick, fixed their breakfast. Mike didn't laugh in the morning. He poured coffee, drank as much as he had time to drink, grabbed a cup of yogurt from the refrigerator and a spoon from the drawer, and hurried to the car by seven-thirty. Sometimes he kissed Tane and told her that he loved her. Sometimes he forgot. Patients would be arriving at the office soon and he had to be there in time to do his paperwork while things were quiet.

As he drove away from the house he often wished he could be more excited about the day like Tane, the optimist. But he was Mike, the optometrist. He carried the weight of two offices, two houses, two children, two dogs, one cat and one wife squarely on his shoulders.

He looked with envy at other professionals who worked four days a week and played golf every Wednesday afternoon. What did they do differently? The few times he carved out for tennis only reminded him of how his game had deteriorated since college. And when he saw himself in the mirror, his was no longer the well-honed body of a regular weightlifter. Softness had attacked him from the middle.

Since they had committed to buying the new house, even Mike's weekend play time, which he spent with Tane and the children, was lost. They had spent all day Saturday and Sunday emptying drawers and cabinets and shelves of their dishes and books and toys, wrapping them with paper and packing them carefully in boxes — sometimes twice after Kaylan or Mick took them out again. The house had become an obstacle course — a shamble, Mike said — of boxes and stuff on the floor awaiting boxes.

Mike's whole life felt like so much stuff sitting on the floor waiting to be organized.

Six

Monday, August 10, 1992
9 a.m.

Bonnell Davis walked from her small brick house under centuries-old oak trees up to the family cemetery at the top of the hill before the heat set in. A soft morning breeze chilled her bare arms and gave just a hint that fall was coming soon. Georgia mountain weather was funny like that. Steamy heat the first few days of August had followed ten inches of July rain. Now the nights were dropping into the low sixties, cool enough for Bonnell and her husband, Sam, to sleep with the windows open.

Bonnell liked to tell people she was an outdoors person, a woman who preferred working in the yard or the garden to keeping house. If she didn't have any outdoor chores, she might walk down the middle of the quiet road in front of the house and listen to the wind in the trees or look for a hawk soaring overhead. Or she might run into her two grandsons stalking squirrels with their pellet guns. Davis Road cut a long, leafy tunnel into the forest and ended at the Etowah River. Nobody came down it except to visit the Davises or to see the colors change in the fall. The cars that did come rolled slowly and stayed in the middle of the road, so weeds crept in from both sides.

The place had hardly changed since Rachel Davis, Sam's Cherokee Indian great-grandmother, looked up at the sky through the same trees. The six-hundred acres of forest and open land surrounding the house had been in Sam's family since the Cherokees were forced out in the 1830s. Following a land lottery, Sam's great-grandfather, Daniel Davis, who had married Rachel a few years earlier, took possession of the tract between the river and Dahlonega. Thirty years later, in 1868, he became the first of the Davis line to be laid to rest in the family cemetery. Whenever Bonnell was depressed, she made the short hike just to feel the spirits of the good people buried there.

She walked up the hill almost every day in early August 1992. Her father had died on July 20, and although he was buried in a churchyard cemetery several miles away, Bonnell knew he was close by each time she stood among the trees and the stones marking several dozen Davises.

Bonnell believed in angels. They watched over her in the cemetery, in the forest surrounding it and in her home. One of her favorite Bible passages was from Psalms, quoted later by Jesus when tempted by Satan: "For He will command His angels concerning you to guard you in all your ways. They will lift you up in their hands so that you will not strike your foot against a stone." She believed so strongly in the celestial beings that for years she collected angel paintings, carvings and figurines, more than fifty in all, placing them on shelves and walls throughout the house. She loved most one she had found in the attic of the old Davis homestead -- a charcoal drawing dated 1882 and titled "To God." It showed an angel, wings spread, cradling a child and carrying her into the night sky, to Heaven. She put it on the wall near the front door where she could see it from the kitchen or the living room.

At the edge of the quarter-acre cemetery Bonnell rubbed her fingers over Daniel and Rachel Davis' mossy stones, so worn by rain and time she could barely read the inscriptions.

Through the trees she heard a car driving toward the highway. Must be the renter going to work. Bonnell felt bad for Donnie Radford. Seemed like he was having a tough time getting back on his feet. Donnie had told her on Friday how he had lost everything in his divorce — his wife, his house, his son, everything. She thought he looked older than his forty years — sagging skin, tired eyes. She was glad she could help him out, and relieved to rent the trailer to someone she knew.

She felt a deep sense of responsibility regarding the trailer. Her daughter and son-in-law, Vera and Mike, and their two young sons lived about twenty yards from it in their partially completed home — a cinder-block basement with a roof. When a previous renter exposed himself to Vera and the boys, Bonnell vowed never to rent to another single man.

Donnie was different. His parents were known in the community, good people, and he had gone to high school with Vera, who didn't know him well but couldn't say anything bad about him. She did remember that the Radfords hadn't always lived in Lumpkin County. Seemed like they'd come from Oregon or someplace like that.

Bonnell was watering a potted pepper plant just outside her back door on Friday afternoon when Donnie drove up. They had made the arrangements earlier, and he was coming by to pay the first month's rent.

"Come on over and have a seat," she said as Donnie stepped out of his car. "I'll go inside and get the key."

Donnie moved slowly and was just settling into a lawn chair when Bonnell came back out.

"I guess you saw the furniture when Sam showed you the trailer," she said, sitting in the other chair. "Do you need anything else? Some linens?"

"Well, I don't have anything," he said. "My wife got it all."

His accent, or lack of one, reminded her that Donnie wasn't from around here, although he had lived nearby for twenty-five years or more.

"So you need some sheets and towels?" she asked.

"If you don't mind," he said. "I'll bring them back when I get a chance to get some of my own."

"Let me go see what I can find," Bonnell said, standing again. She went into the house and came out a few minutes later with two towels and washcloths and a set of sheets with wide pink and white stripes.

"I'm real sorry about the sheets," she said. "They aren't exactly right for a man."

"That's okay," he said. "I won't need them for long."

"Oh, and the pillow's down in the basement," she said. "I'll bring it down to the trailer after church Sunday. By the way, how are your mother and father? I haven't seen them in such a long time."

"Oh, they're fine," Donnie said, reaching into his pocket and pulling out a roll of cash. "Two fifty?"

"That's right," she said. "And a hundred for the deposit."

He counted out three hundred fifty dollars and gave it to her.

"Thank you," she said, walking beside him toward his car. "I hope you like it. It's mighty quiet out here."

Donnie squinted standing in a patch of sunlight beside his dark gray Trans Am. Bonnell thought he hadn't spent much time outside lately.

He reached into his car for a pair of sunglasses and said, "I like it quiet." Quiet enough so nobody would notice if he brought a woman to the trailer against her will.

Seven

Make a joyful noise unto the Lord.
Psalm 100:1

September 1978

If anybody besides James Mills had a Bible in his football locker, he didn't bring it out. Certainly none of the other freshmen risked being singled out a Christian. And yet, if a senior had stood and said, "I'm one," a sizable group might have followed.

Bob Kunkle, a freshman and one of the managers of the football team, would have joined such a following. Bob went to church most Sundays with his family and had sung in choirs since he was four. He sang solos sometimes, his sweet alto voice maturing into a clear tenor almost as high. He enjoyed singing in front of adults and children. But no way would he have stood alone in front of a bunch of football players and sung. Not unless they made him.

Two weeks before school started, Bob traveled with the team to football camp at Mars Hill, North Carolina. There they practiced three times a day, ate every meal together and gathered in a big room at night to talk before going to bed. In addition to maximizing practice time, the routine brought the players together, teaching them to depend on each other. As a manager, Bob looked after equipment and first-aid supplies, and occasionally felt separate from, or even intimidated by, the group. Most of them were older and bigger, and all of them had athletic skills he desired.

Early each morning, Bob made the first footprints on the dewy field, whistling or humming a cheerful chorus of "Beulah Land" as he carried out balls and blocking dummies and extra tape. He thought he was out of earshot, but sound travels far on a Blue Ridge morning. Three practice sessions later, with mountains finally blocking the August sun and the players dragging themselves off the field, he gathered the same equipment and hummed a slow "Swing Low."

By Thursday night, the entire team neared exhaustion. Several of the younger players, who had never been away for a week straight, longed for home. Earlier in the week, when they weren't practicing or eating or sleeping, they had sought mischief — water balloons or fire extinguishers. Now they just sat around and talked. After supper about thirty of them, including Bob, found their way to a big meeting room with a low, acoustical-tile ceiling and fluorescent lights. They sat in three groups. Bob's group, which included James Mills, talked football. Bob didn't say much. Another group discussed girls, and the third planned a poker game. From over his shoulder Bob heard somebody say, "Hey, Bob, sing us a song." He looked back quickly to see who had spoken, and his first thought was, run.

"No, I don't think so," he said, unsure who had spoken, or why.

"Yeah, Bob, you sing great," another voice said. "C'mon."

Were they teasing or did the really think he was good, Bob wondered. Rarely did he pass up an opportunity to sing, but singing to the football team, the guys he lived with and looked up to and who might snicker at him, he just couldn't do that. Besides, what would he sing? A church song? What else did he know?

"Sing, Bob, sing," called a voice from the right.

"Yeah, sing," came another. "Don't be a chicken." And soon the room echoed with demands for a performance.

Bob crossed his legs and his face flushed. "No," he said, "you don't really want me to sing."

But they ignored his plea, drowning it out with their own chorus of, "Sing, Bob, sing."

He was facing a mob which offered no escape.

James, who sat four feet away, then said calmly, "You can do it, Bob."

Bob looked at James and knew he was serious, not teasing. Maybe some of the others felt the same way. Then a voice from the back rose above the noise, "Hey, Bob, what will it take to make you sing?"

Bob finally looked at the team. He would do it. "You have to close the door and turn out the lights," he said. "I can't do it if I have to look at you."

He was committed and his mood immediately shifted from defender to performer. He decided to sing a verse of "Amazing Grace," the only song he could be sure to remember under the pressure. Still, he needed darkness. He couldn't stand to see the guys laughing at him. He put both feet on the floor and faced the front of the room, away from the crowd, waiting. Behind him someone flipped the light switch. He looked over his shoulder at the faces, backlit by the light from the hall.

"Could somebody close the door?" he asked.

An unseen foot kicked the door and it swung around quickly, squeezing the remaining light from the room as it slammed shut. Bob put his hand on the back of his chair, pushed himself up and turned around. He cleared his throat and the talking continued. It suited him fine if everybody talked instead of listening. He would sing and sit down and be done with it. He put his right knee on his chair to steady himself and began.

"Amazing grace, how sweet the sound ..."

He took a breath and the talking had stopped. He heard only silence. He put his right foot back on the floor, squeezed his hands tightly at his side and sang on. Every face must have been turned toward him in the dark.

"... That saved a wretch like me. I once was lost ..."

He finished the first verse, and the words to the second filled his mouth. He had planned to stop here but he kept singing, unable to control his own on-off switch.

" 'Twas grace that taught my heart to fear, and grace my fears relieved ..."

His voice cracked slightly on the high note of "relieved"

and his knees trembled. He closed his eyes and made the black room blacker and pretended he was singing in front of the church at home, seeing the faces of his parents and others who loved him. High above the congregation a cross floated and he followed it upward toward where the angels must be as he sang. He wasn't even trying to remember the words — they were coming automatically, even as tears welled in the corners of his tightly shut eyes. This had never happened when he sang. Never. And all the while his voice grew stronger through the third verse.

"'Tis grace hath brought me safe thus far and grace will lead me home."

He wiped his cheeks and began the final verse, finding his chair again with his knee so he could sit and drop his head as soon as the lights came on. He moved his mouth and listened.

"We've no less days to sing God's praise than when we first begun."

When he finished, several players coughed but the room remained dark. Bob wiped his face again, sat and took a deep breath to settle himself.

☦ ☦ ☦

Steve Kersh, a sophomore wide receiver, sat so still he couldn't feel the bottom and back of the plastic chair molded to the contour of his body. He experienced only one sensation in the dark room, the sound of "Amazing Grace" flowing into his head like water, then pooling somewhere in his chest and rising toward his mouth. Several times while Bob sang Steve cleared his throat.

He closed his eyes and rubbed them when the lights came on, pretending to be blinded the way he might after a movie. He breathed through his mouth to avoid sniffling. At least half the guys were looking down. James broke the tense silence, saying, "That was great, man." Others agreed and several guys stood and stretched. In the shuffling and shifting of chairs, Steve sniffed quickly, stood and put his hands in his pockets. He looked at Bob for the first time, thinking he would say something, but James already had an arm around Bob's shoulder. Steve headed for the door then looked down the hall for the water fountain.

Half an hour later Steve lay on his bed staring at the ceiling. Todd Robson and Daniel Rice sat on the other bed and they all wondered aloud if they could have sung in front of thirty guys. Hoots from the poker game down the hall interrupted their conversation.

"I couldn't do it," Steve said.

"Me neither," Todd said.

"I might could if I could sing," James said. He was standing at the open door. "Mind if I come in?"

Steve sat up on the bed. "Course not," he said.

"C'mon in," Daniel said.

James sat on the end of Steve's bed. "What did you think of that?" he asked.

"Blew me away," Todd said. "Blew everybody away."

"What about you, Steve?" James asked.

Steve felt the point of the question. James must have seen him when the lights came on — he saw that Steve had been moved, maybe even changed. But Steve wasn't ready to commit aloud. Except for his reputation, he hardly knew James, who had moved to Hall County a year earlier.

"Yeah," Steve said. "It was something."

"The Lord blessed Bob with a beautiful voice," James said.

None of the other three would have used the same words, invoking the name of "the Lord" so comfortably. But they all agreed with James, who had a way of making bold statements sound natural and easy to go along with. James talked about "the Lord" a lot, usually in small groups and almost always to people who appeared receptive. He had a way of knowing who wanted to be pushed and who didn't. Steve looked ready to be pushed.

✢ ✢ ✢

Growing up in a devout Christian family, James felt not just a desire but a duty to keep a Bible close by. Every night his family came together around a small altar for prayer and devotion. James' father or mother would read aloud from the Bible, then his father would lay one hand on the altar. James, his brother, sister and mother would then lay their hands on top of the father's, who would put his other hand over theirs and pray. The ritual never became routine for James. Every night the warmth of his family's hands around his, and the strength of his father's prayers, renewed his confidence in their collective bond with God.

He carried that confidence with him each morning, knowing he could speak boldly for God and, no matter who rejected him, the hands would be waiting at home at the altar.

As a fifth grader kneeling at the church altar one Sunday morning, James was overcome by a feeling that God was calling him to preach — not someday when he grew up, but right then. He told the minister, who took his call seriously. The church built a small pulpit for twelve-year-old James to speak from on Sunday nights. He usually told the Old Testament stories he enjoyed most, like David and Goliath or Daniel in the lion's den, and he rarely spoke much longer than ten minutes. His reputation grew to the point that churches around the area invited him to speak.

But the year James entered the eighth grade, his father was transferred to south Hall County and the opportunities to speak publicly waned.

✝ ✝ ✝

Rita Bell, like James Mills, responded to God's touch. She was eleven when she accepted Jesus and felt she owed Him her life. She didn't carry a Bible to school or wear a cross, but from that point on she based most of her decisions on her commitment to Christ.

James and Rita found easy entry into the popular high school crowd through his athletic ability and her genuine beauty. Classmates respected them for their integrity and loyalty. Neither was seen as lacking for friends. But when they started high school and the parties moved from Skate Country to any place where alcohol was available, the invitations dried up. Rita and James were too straight to be any fun at a party. They made people feel uncomfortable. Their strong stands made them appear judgmental.

Tane, who had been so devoted to Rita, hardly mourned their fading friendship. She had new friends who showed her new ways to have fun. Tane was a party girl who only occasionally felt the pangs of guilt for not following a straighter course with Rita.

Rita, on the other hand, missed Tane. For three years they had passed notes in class, spent the night over at each other's houses, read the Bible together, shared their deepest secrets. Now Tane had secrets she dared not share with Rita — secrets Rita didn't want to know.

✝ ✝ ✝

Before Tane could drive, her mother would drop her off at the gym for school dances. But Tane didn't always go straight inside. Instead, she and Alecia and Kim and Andrea would meet one of the sixteen-year-old girls with a car in the parking lot. They would all pile in and giggle and talk about boys.

Invariably, one of the girls would say, "Hey, let's go get some wine."

Tane remembered the first time it happened. "Yeah, yeah, party," she said. In fact, the idea scared her. She didn't want to get kicked out of school. But the dare was on the table and Tane had added momentum. The sixteen-year-old driver took her load of silly acting girls to a package store on Browns Bridge Road, where they gave a man outside five dollars to buy them a bottle of Boone's Farm Strawberry Hill wine.

Fortunately the top screwed off, for none of the girls had, or knew how to use, a corkscrew. Tane took a drink when her turn came — sweet, not too bad — then passed the bottle on. They snickered as the wine made its way around the car. One girl tried to remember a drinking game her brother had told her about but she couldn't get it right.

They drove to the Dairy Mart parking lot, across the road from the gym, where they passed the bottle one more time, then they all piled out to go to the bathroom. A third of the sugary stuff remained, but the girls had had enough. Tane dropped the bottle in the trash can. Still laughing, they climbed back into the car and drove over to the dance.

Tane was slightly buzzed when she climbed out of the car with her friends and walked toward the gym. The fresh autumn night chilled her flush cheeks. Hoping none of the teachers would suspect what they'd been up to, she walked carefully in her high heels. Barely five feet tall, Tane wore heels almost every day in high school, even with blue jeans, which she wore with a sweater for the dance.

That night began a tradition of sorts. The girls often would meet in somebody's car before a dance or on a Saturday night with nothing going on and pass around a bottle of wine. They liked breaking the rules and almost never got in trouble. Except for that one time.

Tane was riding in the back seat when they saw the blue lights. The car load of boys and girls had been cruising and drinking. A couple of the guys had even shared a joint. This is it, Tane thought. Big trouble.

The policeman walked up to the car. "You know how fast you were going?" he asked.

Nobody spoke until Alecia or somebody said, "We're sorry, sir. We were just riding around talking.

"Okay," the policeman said, "everybody out and into the back seat of the patrol car — all of you."

Five teenagers spilled out of the car and into the police car, scared, shaking, going to jail. Tane had never ridden in a police car. A steel cage separated the back seat from the front and there were no handles on the back door. She was in until somebody let her out. When they did, she would have to call her mother to come get her. She fought back tears as the car turned toward Gainesville.

"You know, there's a lot of kids like you, good kids, getting into trouble these days," the policeman said. "They do things that get them put in jail and they don't realize how much they hurt their parents and how much they mess themselves up for a long time to come. Have you ever thought about what it would be like to have your mamas and daddies have to pick you up at the jail? Have you ever considered how much you'd be letting them down?"

As the policeman talked, Tane decided to call Mama Dese from jail instead of her mother. But the policeman didn't go to jail with his load. He never accused them directly of breaking the law. He just gave them a taste of what it would be like if they did — a chance to think about the consequences. When he dropped them off back at the car, they all went straight home. Tane lay in bed thinking how lucky she was and wondering if God had kept her out of jail. She prayed for the first time in weeks, thanking Him for delivering her home secretly.

When the preacher stood up on Sunday and talked about being ready for Jesus to return because the hour was at hand, Tane knew he was talking about her. The policeman had been a sign. A warning. The preacher told about the man who ate and drank with drunkards and was sent off with the hypocrites, "where there will be wailing and gnashing of teeth."

Tane had to straighten up or she'd be right there, too.

"Watch, therefore," the preacher said, "for you do not know what hour your Lord will return."

☩ ☩ ☩

By Monday morning Tane's guilt had abated considerably. It was a school day, and on school days it was more important to be popular than to be a devoted Christian, no matter what she had promised on Friday night. It would take something bigger than a ride in a police car to scare Tane straight. She woke with the six o'clock alarm, giving her enough time to shower and fix her hair and makeup. As a freshman Tane was already a walking temptation and she knew it. Senior boys always checked out freshmen girls the first week of school, and at Johnson High School Tane was one they watched closely. When she walked down the hall at school she smiled and spoke to each person, making sure that every boy and every girl liked her. She had been voted Miss South Hall by her eighth-grade class the year before, and she intended to remain the most popular. To prove her popularity to herself, Tane had to be the first girl asked out by any a new boy who moved to town. If he was cute, that is. She knew how to flirt — how to let them know she was interested. And time after time — Dusty, Bobby, Kent — she was the first one they called.

Eight

*Some [seed] fell on rocky places where it did not have much
soil. It sprang up quickly, because the soil was shallow. But
when the sun came up, the plants were scorched, and they
withered because they had no root.*
— Matthew 13:5-6

September 1979

Milton and Brenda Robson married right out of high
school, starting with almost no money. Milton sold meat from
a freezer truck to restaurants in Gainesville and across the
north Georgia mountains every day while Brenda and her
mother stayed home grinding, wrapping and freezing sau-
sage or making hamburger patties. Milton would then work
late into the night checking his receipts against his order tickets
before he finally took off his cowboy boots for the day.

The attractive young couple had not yet laid a financial
foundation when Todd was born in 1962, and they struggled
on. Two years later Brenda gave birth to a daughter. Milton,
still the cowboy, had read an article about Doug McClure,
the actor who played Trampas on the TV western *The Vir-
ginian*, and McClure's daughter, Tane. He liked the unusual
name, and so did Brenda, so they gave it to their tiny, dark-
haired, dark-eyed baby girl.

Milton turned back to his business where, for the next
five years, he worked without another employee, making con-
tacts and earning a reputation for quality products. Later, as
Todd and Tane grew from children into teenagers, their father expanded the company exponentially until Milton's Institutional Foods became a multimillion dollar enterprise.

Milton often worked fourteen-hour days as the company
grew, although Tane never felt she lacked for his attention. In
her eyes theirs was a perfect family. Brenda had grown up
going to church every Sunday, but Milton had not. When the
children were old enough, one of the parents would drop them

off for Sunday School, then go home and come back to sit with them in church.

Not until she was a teenager did Tane consider how much they had — the big house, the classic car collection. People said her father was one of the richest men in the county. But in her eyes he didn't act rich. He still wore blue jeans and cowboy boots to work. Both of her parents had grown up country and they stayed country, never becoming members of society's elite in nearby Gainesville. And her father almost never handed out extra cash to her or Todd. "You need to work and earn your money," he said, "to know where it comes from."

That's the way Tane liked it. She wanted the independence of earning her own money. So her mother dropped her off at Dunaway Drugs in College Square every weekday morning during the summer of 1979. A year away from getting her driver's license, Tane straightened the merchandise on shelves, worked the cash register, swept or did whatever else Mr. Hess, the manager, needed, for the minimum wage.

Hank Hess admired Tane's hard work. Not many teenagers he hired anymore were as dependable. And she was so friendly. When she worked the check-out, she struck up a conversation with almost every customer. Older women told Hess "what a nice young girl" she was. Teenage boys lingered especially long, for Tane, at fifteen, already had grown-up curves they were drawn to.

From across the parking lot Donnie Radford, the twenty-six-year-old manager of Jack's Hamburgers, walked to Dunaway Drugs once or twice a week, lingering and stealing long looks at Tane when her head was turned, sometimes spending several minutes buying a pack of gum.

"Hey there," Tane would say when he was finally ready to pay. It was her standard customer greeting and usually elicited a similar response.

The man's silent interest in her was obvious to others who worked there, although Tane never noticed. His visits ended in September when she started her sophomore year in high school.

✝ ✝ ✝

Increasingly, Tane had heard friends talk about their parents' affairs and split-ups. Now her best friend was telling her a rumor that her own father was seeing another woman. Worst of all, her friend said Tane's parents were divorcing. That's what really upset Tane. She was hearing about her parents' breakup for the first time at school. Tane couldn't believe nobody had told her first.

She turned sixteen less than a year after the divorce, and she knew what her father planned to give her for a birthday present. The Corvette. He had bought the 1975 yellow convertible five years earlier for his collection, which by that time was up to about forty cars. He told Tane he thought she would look good in it, so in April, when she got her driver's license, he gave it to her.

He was right. Tane did look good in it — even resembled it. The car's sleek, fiberglass body, the color of a caution light, wrapped tightly around a muscular engine. The long, slender hood rode so low that the front fenders had to curve upward and back down again to make room for the tires. And the interior resembled a cockpit, slightly cramped, with an automatic stick shift between two leather seats.

Tane sat low in the driver's seat and headed for the highway, the top down, her hair in a ponytail blowing straight back, and country music blaring from the stereo.

That was the year Tane's parents became her "friends." She lived with her mother, who picked up the pieces of her shattered marriage and started dating again. On weekend mornings they would trade stories like schoolgirls, which Tane still was. She felt grown up. Neither of her parents was as strict as they had been before, and Tane took advantage of the opportunity to party.

Almost every weekend somebody's parents left town for a couple of nights. Word spread fast among the cool crowd at

Johnson High School, and by Saturday night the parentless home was well represented by laughing and drinking and dancing and kissing teenagers, Tane among them. If she didn't have a date, she'd get a couple of girls to ride with her, one of them squeezing behind the seats or sitting on the back of the two-seater homecoming-queen style. They'd share a bottle of wine and talk about who would be together at the party. Then they'd talk about which boys were the best kissers. If Alecia or Kim said so-and-so was the best and Tane had never kissed him, she'd make plans to correct the situation right away. The other girls would do the same — it became a game to them — and they would compare notes after the party. Tane rarely failed in her efforts to kiss the selected boy, for Tane was the kind of girl boys liked to kiss.

In fact, most boys wanted to do a lot more than kiss Tane. Every time she had dated a boy for a couple of months, he would begin to pressure her for more. The idea didn't excite Tane, but sometimes she gave in.

Lying in bed on a Sunday morning, hungover and all alone, Tane realized how totally lost she was. She had drunk so much the night before she couldn't remember where she had been, what she had done or how she had gotten there. She had done things with boys she liked, maybe even loved. But now, in the light of morning, she wanted to undo everything — to turn back the clock 24 hours and live the day again, only this time without the drinking and everything that went with it. Then, instead of going to church, she went downstairs and drank coffee with her mother as they discussed their evening. Tane held back some of her details — often because she didn't remember all the details. On some Sundays, before she went downstairs, Tane reached for her Bible and read a few verses just to make a connection. It was Sunday, after all, and she still yearned, at least occasionally, for some kind of relationship with God.

Later they might go to Mama Dese's and Daddy Cliff's house. If Dese had asked Tane what she had done on Saturday night, she might have confessed, but Dese rarely asked Tane hard questions. Instead, she left her Bible on the coffee table in the living room, she went to church every Sunday morning and evening and prayer meeting on Wednesday, and she always wrapped her arms around Tane and said, "I love you, honey."

Going to Dese's house was like climbing back into her mother's womb. She didn't want to leave, to breathe independently and face the world's disappointments. She wanted instead to shrink into her grandmother's lap and listen to a Bible story. "Tell me the stories of Jesus ..." She wanted to run through the cemetery with Daddy Cliff and hear him read the Lord's Prayer. "Lead us not into temptation, but deliver us from evil ..." She didn't have to decide right and wrong when she was with Dese and Cliff. They decided and they were always right and she could follow them. They made it easy to be good. She didn't want to leave. She didn't want to have to decide for herself. She so often decided wrong.

✝ ✝ ✝

James Mills prayed daily for a spiritual revival at Johnson High School. Every Monday in the hall or in the locker room before baseball practice he heard about the weekend parties — who drank how much, who woke up where, which guys slept with which girls. He never repeated the stories of conquest, but neither did he forget them. Instead, he laid them aside for later consideration. His recollections saddened him, sometimes for the guys who sought their pleasure immorally and sometimes for himself because he had chosen to be left out.

When he felt tempted to join in the talk, he would go to his locker, open his Bible discretely and read from Romans 12: "Offer your bodies as living sacrifices, holy and pleasing to God. This is your spiritual act of worship. Do not conform any longer to the pattern of this world, but be transformed by the renewing of your mind."

James' back straightened, lifting him slightly taller as he

closed his Bible and placed it back in his locker. The words that strengthened him could change his whole school if people would listen to them. He might have stood in the hall and in the locker room and shouted them himself, but James knew that being branded a religious nut would diminish his effectiveness as a messenger. People respected him as a varsity athlete and a person true to his convictions — a good example even if they didn't invite him to their parties. God would give him a chance to make a difference.

Then came the night he was at home and Rev. Fulton Boswell called. The preacher at Poplar Springs Baptist Church said they were planning a youth revival and he knew of James' reputation. He wondered if James would speak all three nights.

This was it, James thought as a lightness filled and lifted him. Here was his chance, and he was willing to summon the courage. He didn't even need to pray for an answer. Yes, indeed, he would speak.

✝ ✝ ✝

When word got out that James Mills was preaching a three-night revival at Poplar Springs, her church, Tane felt a stirring. She had always loved revivals, even though she hadn't been to one in years. Revivals reminded her of her grandmother and made her feel like a little girl. The singing, the informal friendliness, the fresh voice of a visiting preacher, the excitement of the spirit sweeping through the church and moving people to laughter or tears lifted and inspired her.

She was seven years old when Mama Dese took her to her first revival at Pleasant Hill Baptist Church. The memory of reaching up to hold her grandmother's cool, dry hand as they walked down the aisle, then kneeling at the altar for the first time still stirred her.

Tane wanted to walk down the aisle again. She wanted to plant a seed that would grow deep and strong. She would do it in front of all her friends, really commit herself, if they would go down the aisle too — if James would lead them to do it. She couldn't go alone. She would look weird if she stood all by herself in front of the church and recommitted her life to Christ. Her party friends would have to go with her. Not just Rita and Kathy and Steve, who, everybody knew, were Christians. It was up to James to get the others there. She believed he could do it. Lots of people liked him, and almost everybody respected him. He could stand up and say he was a Christian and be a regular guy too.

Tane took it upon herself to get her friends there, while taking care not to over commit herself. "Hey, why don't we go listen to James next week," she'd say. "I've never heard a teenager preach before."

Almost everybody she asked said yes. Tane had more pull than she realized. Plus, being a "group Christian" wasn't that hard. Sunday night came and dozens of teenagers — James' football and baseball teammates, several cheerleaders, lots of the cool crowd — filed into the red brick church at dusk. Tane's yellow Corvette parked out front announced to all that she was already inside. Other than that, she stayed unusually quiet, mixing in with a big group of girls she had invited sitting on the right side of the aisle. James and Rev. Boswell sat in chairs behind the pulpit. They were the only ones in the church wearing suits.

After some songs and announcements, throughout which the girls whispered and passed notes they wrote on offering envelopes, Rev. Boswell introduced James, who stood and walked slowly, with his back perfectly straight, to the pulpit. He read from the Old Testament book of Daniel and he sounded just like a real preacher. He was so calm, Tane couldn't believe it.

Then he preached about Shadrach, Meshach and Abednego, the Jewish boys who refused to worship the golden statue made by Babylonian King Nebuchadnezzar and were thrown into the fiery furnace. But they walked around in the furnace and the flames never hurt them. God protected them.

God had commanded them not to worship that golden idol, James told his congregation, and when the king tried to make them bow down, God protected them. Too often, he continued, people today bow down to their "images of gold" — money, cars, even their own popularity — putting those things before God. When the fiery furnace of tribulation engulfs them, they don't have God at their side to help.

James made it sound so clear, so simple. Tane wanted God at her side. She wanted to put Him first.

James finished, then invited anyone to come to the front and lay on the altar, figuratively, of course, any gods that came between them and the one true God. He was the first to kneel. Several teenagers and adults, tears on their cheeks, came to pray beside him. Tane slid across the pew to the aisle and fell into the flow. As the people knelt, Rev. Boswell stood at the pulpit and asked, "Is there anyone here who feels like the Lord has something on their hearts? Please speak up."

With that, Tane's brother, Todd, stood from where he knelt at the altar, turned toward the congregation, and said, "James has shown us what we can truly be." His voice cracked with emotion. "I say let's win Johnson High School for Christ. Let's share Him with our friends."

The words shocked Tane. Todd partied even more than she did. But there he was, speaking out.

Hank Bond stood and seconded Todd's motion. This was exactly what Tane was hoping for — regular people standing up for Christ. Now she could speak. She stood at the altar and proclaimed that she was recommitting her life to Christ. A dozen more followed as the atmosphere inside the sanctuary changed from worship service to pep rally with hoots and hollers.

Rev. Boswell invited anybody who wanted to stay to come to the fellowship hall to talk more about what was happening. Tane joined the group of about twenty who said they would like to meet every week. James said he would lead the group, which dubbed itself Christseekers, after the television show Thrillseekers, and Rev. Boswell said they could gather at the church on Saturday nights.

For several weeks the group grew, as teenagers skipped parties to hear James talk about the rapture and the afterlife. Tane read her Bible almost every night, and she stopped drinking and partying.

Then summer came. Christseekers disbanded until September and the party was on again. With no weekly gatherings for three months, the embers scattered so far they never came together again. Tane still picked up her Bible occasionally, and if she saw a sign in front of a church for a revival she might go alone, hoping to rekindle the spirit within her. But the lure of the party and the need to maintain her popularity doused the flicker.

Nine

*Because you are lukewarm, and neither cold nor hot, I will
spew you out of My mouth.*
— Revelation 3:16

Monday, August 10, 1992
9 a.m.

Thirteen years later Tane's spark for Christ lay buried
under years of ashes. She and Mike attended church, and she
had even volunteered at Vacation Bible School. She wanted
Kaylan and Mick at least to be exposed to church. But on
Sunday Tane looked forward to Monday, when she could get
back to the gym and teach her aerobics class, a priority second
only to the children.

After Mike left for work and she started load of laundry,
she put on her workout clothes, black, to-the-knee stretch
pants and a matching sports bra, plus shorts and a tank top
for the trip into town. Monday and Thursday were extra
aerobics days at Gold's Gym. Tane preceded her regular high-
impact aerobics class with a notoriously tough forty-five-
minute workout of slow squats and steps that burned every
muscle below the waist.

The hardest part of her day was getting out of the house.
She put a fresh diaper on Mick and dressed him, then helped
Kaylan with her shoes.

"Let's go play at Gold's," she said as they went downstairs, Mick on her left hip and Kaylan following closely.

With her free arm Tane moved the first load of clothes
from the washer to the dryer and started the second load washing.

"Honey, could you make sure the sliding glass door is
locked?" she asked Kaylan as she circled the kitchen turning
off the coffee pot, checking the oven and putting dirty dishes
in the dishwasher. She watched as Kaylan tried to push open
the door to the deck.

"It's locked, Mommy."

Tane grabbed her gym bag off a chair at the kitchen table, and they walked through to the front door, locked it, and finally headed back through the den and out the door to the garage. Tane loaded the children into their car seats, climbed in and backed out of the driveway. Mick pointed and said "trees," and when they came to the red light at Thompson Bridge Road he pointed again and said "top!"

"That's right," Tane said. "Red light means stop."

When they got to Gold's and stepped inside, Tane was relieved to hear children's voices coming from the yellow and orange nursery. Kaylan usually wouldn't cry if she had somebody to play with.

"Y'all have fun and I'll be back in a little bit," Tane said as she put Mick down.

In the aerobics room Tane stepped out of her lime green jogging shorts and pulled her navy blue tank top over her head. She bent down to adjust her athletic socks and glanced at her image in the wall-size mirror. Not bad for a twenty-eight-year-old mother of two. The stretch pants and sports bra hid none of her curvy figure and even enhanced the tan on her flat tummy and her tight shoulders and arms. She stuffed her shorts and tank top into her gym bag and found an elastic band. Two men in the adjoining weight room, separated by a glass wall and door, relaxed from their workouts to watch as she threaded her thick dark hair into a long ponytail.

She checked and adjusted the sound level on the tape player as the door opened. "Hey, Jennifer. Hey, Lisa," she said to the first of her Monday morning class members. "How are y'all doing?"

"Hi, Tane," they said in unison.

Three more women followed closely, and the rest of the class made their way through the weight room. Each woman followed a pre-workout routine similar to Tane's, engaging in small talk as they went.

"Ready?" Tane asked after they had formed two rows.

"Let's go," a couple of the women said.

Tane cranked up the music and started them easy with warm-up bending and loosening. The moves were automatic. These were Tane's extra aerobics regulars, forever endeavoring to head off any out-of-place dimples. They all knew the routine. Quickly she guided them into their agonizingly slow knee bends and steps.

"Burning yet?" Tane asked. She knew they were because she was, and she pushed them further until their thigh muscles nearly tore out of their skin. After thirty minutes they watched the clock as much as they watched Tane, hoping they could hang on until the end.

As tight and tired as they were, most of the women stayed for Tane's aerobics class, which would stretch the muscles they had just tightened, and eight more women joined them.

In the few minutes between classes Jennifer Kowalske told Tane she was taking her boys to get a haircut later in the day and said they might drop by her house to visit.

"Come on by," Tane said. "Mick will be napping, but Kaylan can play with Rusty and Zack and we can talk. The house is a wreck 'cause we're trying to get packed to move."

She looked up at the clock. "Okay, line 'em up," she said as she turned the music back on, and she was going again. "Let's stretch out those weekend kinks."

All of the women followed her lead, pivoting to the left and bending one knee to stretch their quadriceps. Tane's back was to her class so they could more easily mimic her moves. Watching them in the big mirror, she stepped up, down and around a small plastic platform, yelling instructions in a language unique to aerobics. "Here we go ... V-step, six, five, four ... Now travel step around back and heel, toe, heel, toe ..."

Tane's ponytail swung from side to side and slapped her back as she accelerated into the routine. "C'mon, Lisa, you're dragging!"

After fifteen minutes, Tane's skin glistened as if it had

been oiled. Huge drops of sweat rolled off the elbows and noses of some of her followers. This was why they took Tane's class — to sweat. They weren't Atlanta hardbody types, but the women were in shape and Tane kept them that way. She shifted into overdrive, kicking and turning and bending and sliding. As she drove them through their final steps, several of the women ran visibly low on gas. Some gasped for air as sweat spots on their leotards grew larger. Tane began cool-down stretches and the heavy breathing women smiled with relief. She and her pupils applauded themselves when they finished the session, and Tane felt lighter as she walked through the wide-open weight room, through the lobby and to the nursery. She would just peek in to be sure Kaylan and Mick were all right.

"Mommy! Mommy!" Kaylan cried when she caught sight of her mother. Tane should have stayed in the other room.

"I just came to check on you, honey," she said. "Play with Mick and let Mommy go work out a little longer and we'll go to Mama Dese's house for lunch."

Tane steeled herself to Kaylan's cries, which she could hear all the way back into the weight room, but she had to do it.

Four times a week Tane followed her class with a weightlifting session, which she enjoyed even more than aerobics. Her class made her focus on the other women instead of her own workout. The relative solitude of the weight room on a Monday morning allowed her to concentrate on her body — to push her muscles to their limits and feel them straining against the weight of the bars. She worked mainly with free weights, the ones body builders used, instead of weightlifting machines. Free weights gave her muscles greater tone and definition. Plus she liked the simplicity of just her and the weights, not a bunch of gears and cables on a machine.

When she finished her workout, she hurried to the locker room and changed into her shorts and tank top, washed her face, then ran to the nursery to get Kaylan and Mick.

"Come on, guys," she said. "Let's go see Mama Dese and Grandmother."

Kaylan jumped up and ran over to her mother while Mick climbed from his all-fours to his feet and half-ran, half-staggered across the room. Tane picked up Mick, who was up to about twenty-five pounds, and carried him in her left arm, reaching down with her right to hold Kaylan's hand as they walked out into the middle of August.

Tane opened the door of her bright red Jeep Cherokee and heat boiled out like lava from a volcano. She buckled Mick in as quickly as she could and helped Kaylan situate herself in front, then she ran around so she could start the engine and the air conditioner. Sweat finally popped out in big, heavy drops on her face and arms as she reached for the "MAX" button and the cool air blew on her. She adjusted the vents to make sure Mick got plenty of air in the back seat.

Mama Dese lived on the other side of town, but the bypass around the downtown business district made the drive easy. Tane cut through a neighborhood of brick houses on big grassy lots that eventually gave way to heavy woods and steep ridges. This was where the Blue Ridge Mountains ran out of steam, on the western edge of Gainesville, Georgia, at the shores of Lake Lanier. Although she had grown up out in the county, Tane knew these streets and hills well. In high school she had cruised them with her friends on weekend nights. Now they made her think of Mike. Gainesville was Mike's town. He had grown up here, the son of a prominent and popular optometrist. He had played high school tennis well enough to earn a college scholarship, and most of the girls at Gainesville High would have dated with him if he had asked. But he was too shy.

Mike was the only real boyfriend Tane ever had — the only one she said "I love you" to and meant it. Now the spark was fading. Always the kids. Always Mike's work. Then on weekends they spent every minute with Kaylan and Mick. Never alone. They were drifting apart. Slowly. It would take years. She knew it. He didn't. They had shared a passion for fitness. They had worked out in the weight room together or run five or six miles through these neighborhoods, over these hills, talking and laughing and pushing each other to their physical limits. So long ago.

She drove down a hill, turned left onto Chestatee Road and drove past Wilshire Trails Park.

"Slide! Slide!" Mick screamed when he caught sight of the park.

"No, honey, we're going to Mama Dese's right now," Tane answered.

"Slide!"

"We'll go to the park tomorrow and slide."

Wilshire Trails, layered thick with the previous fall's yellow-brown leaves of poplar, birch, maple and oak, wound for more than half a mile along a rocky stream at the base of a sheer ridge that rose so high it blocked the sun until midday. Most important, the park had colorful plastic slides that spun like a corkscrew or bounced up and down or zipped straight down through a big tube. And it had swings and a giant sand box. At least twice a week Tane and five other mothers met at McDonald's with their children, then went to the park to play. At eighteen months, Mick had just outgrown his fear of the slides, as long as his mother slid down with him, and he wanted to slide every day. Tane accelerated to get the park out of sight and out of Mick's mind, driving up the hill past the mall and on to Mama Dese's house.

The ritual of Monday lunch with Mama Dese began when Tane was pregnant with Kaylan and she was working at her father's company. She had lost her first child to a miscarriage when she was thirteen weeks pregnant, and was feeling nauseous in her second pregnancy.

"Come over to the house," Dese said when Tane called her on a Monday morning for sympathy, "and I'll try to fix something you can eat."

Dese must have been worried about Tane getting enough

because she worked all morning cooking fried chicken and fried okra and squash and tomatoes and cornbread. Tane mostly picked at her food, but the cornbread tasted good to her. They ate at the kitchen table with Daddy Cliff, who was there in body and spirit. His mind had slowly left him some years earlier. His granddaughter and his wife were familiar to him, but he couldn't quite place them. Kaylan and Mick would never know Daddy Cliff as the man who ran through the cemetery with their mother.

After they had lunch together that first Monday morning, Mama Dese invited Tane back the next week and the next, and they decided they had created a tradition. Mama Dese thought it would be fun to expand the circle, so she invited Todd and his wife and Sherri and Brenda. Daddy Cliff was the only one at the table who didn't talk much, although he brightened when his great-grandchildren came in the room and when everybody else laughed. After Kaylan and Mick were born, conversation almost always centered on them, unless Mama Dese's sister Pat joined them. Then they talked about God.

"Praise God," Aunt Pat would say as soon as she saw Tane. "Tell me what you've done for the Lord today?"

Tane usually had to think hard to come up with a satisfactory answer, and she hoped Aunt Pat would move on to somebody else during the awkward silence. Mama Dese often rescued her by stepping in and greeting Aunt Pat with a hug.

Ten

You are full of all kinds of deceit and trickery.
— *Acts 13:10*

August 10, 1992
11:30 a.m.

"Not much to look at," Ronnie Wilson said of the two-tone, fourteen-year-old Granada as the screen door of Latimer's Grocery Store slapped behind him, "but she'll run just fine." His customer, wearing too-tight tennis shorts, tube socks and t-shirt, all the color of his pasty skin, had been attracted by the $500 sign painted with shoe polish on the windshield.

Latimer's was an old-fashioned independent grocery store, the kind some people updated and called a "superette" in the Sixties. Well situated on the main highway to Athens until the interstate was built nearby, Latimer's traded on tradition, offering charge accounts and conversation at a table near the register. The tan brick building with small, double-hung windows backed up to an industrial area with massive oil storage tanks across the railroad tracks. Four gasoline pumps stood out front under the round blue-and-white Pure sign, and a truck lift rose from oily dirt around on the side. Harold Latimer had been in the used car business, and still had one or two out front occasionally. The Granada had been there for two weeks.

The man in the shorts walked around the car, leaning over to touch the fender and kicking the tires with his tennis shoes. Wilson, who was Harold Latimer's son-in-law and manager of the store, had seen him walking down from Burger King. Not the kind of person he expected to see in this neighborhood. He was dressed for the lake. The man wasn't saying anything, even when Wilson introduced himself. Wilson put his hands on his hips and watched. It was too hot for this. He turned to go inside to the air conditioner.

52

"Let me know if you're interested," he said.

"Let's crank it and let me hear it run," the man said, and Wilson turned back and gave him the key. The man cranked the engine, pulled the hood release and stepped out. He raised the hood and gazed in, but didn't touch anything.

"Let me check the transmission," he said. He got back in the car, put his foot on the brake and put the car in reverse, then drive. He turned off the ignition and stepped back out.

"You've got a good hundred-dollar car here," he said. "What will you take for it?"

"Well, I tell you," Wilson said. "It's too hot to stand around out here, so just to get right down to business, three-seventy-five is the minimum price that I can cancel it for."

The man thought for a minute then said, "Okay, throw ten dollars worth of gas in it and I'll take it."

The man eased the car to the gas pump and sat while Wilson put in the gas and washed the price off the windshield. The man pulled a roll of cash out of his pocket, counted out nineteen twenty-dollar bills, which looked to be less than half the roll. Wilson wished he had held out for more.

"What about the gas?" Wilson said.

"I meant for you to throw that in," the man responded.

"That's not what I meant."

Without another word the man pulled the roll back out and found a five.

Wilson pulled the tag receipt out of his pocket and said, "Let me write a bill of sale. What's your name?"

"No," the man said. "I don't need a bill of sale. The tag receipt will be fine."

"Okay," Wilson said as the man got into the car. "You know, you put a coat of paint on it and you'll have something you can drive for awhile."

"Not going to use it that much," the man said. He closed the door, rolled down the window and drove toward the Burger King. He needed some things out of his Trans-Am, which he'd left parked there. Then he headed across town toward the Shannons' home.

Eleven

You will call upon me and come and pray to me and I will listen to you.
—Jeremiah 29:12

August 10, 1992
11:30 a.m.

Tane wasn't home yet. She and the children were just arriving at Mama Dese's house for lunch. Kaylan ran in and hugged her grandmother while Tane walked in with Mick. Mama Dese had fixed a cool lunch, ham and potato salad with sliced tomatoes, cucumbers and onions. Kaylan stared out the glass door and said she wanted to eat outside by the pool, but Tane convinced her to stay inside with the air conditioning. She and Mick went to the den and ate in front of the TV while the adults stayed in the kitchen and discussed the early stages of Mick's potty training.

Mick followed his usual schedule. At about one o'clock his eyelids began to droop. And Kaylan, who hadn't taken a nap in over a year, acted sleepy too. She had stayed up late on Saturday and Sunday nights while Mike and Tane packed, and the whole family was up early Monday morning.

"I'd better get these two home before I have to carry both of them," Tane said. She loaded them back in the Jeep and Mick immediately fell asleep. Before they got home Kaylan's eyes and head fell too.

Tane pulled the Jeep into the garage and came around to lift Mick out first. He sighed heavily and his soft little face nestled into her neck and left shoulder as she fumbled with the keys and unlocked the door to the house. She hurried through the den and up the stairs, her thighs tightening and burning slightly after her workout, so she could get back before Kaylan woke up alone in the car. She laid him in his crib and pulled a light blanket over him, closed his door on her way out. Kaylan still slept, so Tane lifted her out, taking care not to bump her head, and carried her to the sofa in the den.

She heard a knock on the door just as she stood up. Jennifer and the boys were there. Surely Kaylan would wake up now.

"Where's Kaylan and Mick?" Rusty asked before Jennifer could even say hello.

"They're sleeping," Tane said. "Let's all go to the living room so they don't wake up."

Furnished almost exclusively with toys and games and children's books, the Shannons' living room was no place for quiet reflection. Tane let the kids run wide-open in there. She loved watching Kaylan and Mick laugh and play. Most of the time she played with them, chasing or being chased and tickled. She closed the double door with the Kowalske boys on the loose, and she and Jennifer settled on the floor.

Jennifer wanted to hear about Milton's surprise birthday party on Saturday night, and Tane was ready to tell the story. For his fiftieth birthday, Milton's family had rented the Georgia Mountains Center downtown and filled it with friends. Jason D. Williams, who played the piano with his hands and elbows and feet like Jerry Lee Lewis, cranked up the crowd and flirted with Tane. She liked the attention at first, but then he came on to her so strongly and publicly that she thought Mike might lose his temper, especially when people started teasing about it. Mike said it was all part of the act, and it probably was.

Kaylan and Mick were still sleeping when Jennifer and the boys left half an hour later. The phone rang and Tane grabbed it on the first ring. Her mother was putting together a silk flower arrangement for Mike's office and wanted to talk about it.

Tane enjoyed talking with her mother, which was good because they usually talked at least three times a day. Brenda called every morning just to check in, then they discussed the daily routine once or twice as it unfolded. When they agreed on the flowers, Tane hung up and, feeling an afternoon sinking spell coming on, made a cup of instant cappuccino. She unloaded the drier and went to the big chair in the den to fold laundry. The still slightly warm clothes felt good on her legs, especially the kids' cotton t-shirts. Folding clothes reminded her again how fast the children were growing. Kaylan, at three-and-a-half, was two years older than Mick, and Tane had to think hard to imagine her daughter fitting into Mick's little shirts and shorts. She gazed at her little girl sleeping on the sofa, tan from summer days at the pool, so small but no longer a baby. Kaylan was smaller than other girls her age, like her mother had been. Also like her mother, she had seemingly boundless energy and bright eyes that sparkled when she smiled. They both smiled a lot.

Tane leaned over to pick up more clothes to fold. As she straightened up, she glanced out the window in the door to the garage and saw the top of a man's head behind her Jeep in the driveway. Must be Leroy Orr, she thought. An older man, Mr. Orr did yard work around the neighborhood and usually wore a straw hat. She thought the toboggan he was wearing must be hot. She put the clothes from her lap onto the floor and stood up to meet him at the door as he stepped into the garage. He had just cut the grass a few days earlier. What could he want?

She looked down at Kaylan as she passed, hoping she could reach the door before Mr. Orr knocked and woke her. Looking up again she saw that the man had pulled the blue and yellow toboggan down over his face like a big sock. She ran to lock the door, and in the second it took her to reach it, she imagined all the things the man in the mask would do to her and her children. If she could slow him with the lock, she could hide the children in a closet and find the gun Mike had hidden in the bedroom or in a drawer or somewhere. She was too late. The man had already turned the knob and was pushing the door open as Tane hit it with her shoulder and pushed with her legs, the words "no, no, no" spewing from her gut. Then she saw the gun, a big silver revolver. It might have been a toy, like one Jennifer's boys would play with, but a second look told her it was real. The gun scared her into backing away; the surgical glove on the hand holding the gun almost made her heave in revulsion. She couldn't scream, no matter what he did to her, for that would risk bringing Kaylan and Mick into the situation.

"You're coming with me," he said, pointing the gun at Tane's stomach. She couldn't see his mouth. He had cut only two ragged holes from which his eyes peered, bright blue, almost hard looking. But the whites were not white. They were soft and yellowish and streaked with red.

He might rape me, he might even kill me, Tane thought, but don't let this be some maniac who kills my kids too. She started figuring a way out.

"Don't kill us," she said, barely above a whisper. "Please don't touch my children."

"I'm not here to hurt you," he answered, just as quietly, "and I won't hurt your kids. I'm just here for money."

They didn't have much money in the house.

"I do my husband's deposits," she said. "I think I might have some upstairs."

"I'm not here for that," he said. "I'm after real money." Tane immediately thought, this guy knows Daddy.

"You want me to call my father?" she said.

"No," he said. "Get some more clothes. We'll be gone awhile. I'm holding you for ransom."

"Don't take my kids," Tane said. "You don't need to take my kids."

"Just you," he said. "Now come on, we got to hurry. Get your stuff."

Tane turned toward the stairs and the man put the gun in her back. Through her tank top the circle of the barrel pressed against her skin and ribs. Terrified, she walked carefully so that neither she nor the man would stumble. Kaylan slept on the sofa as they passed. Mike wouldn't be home until eight, five more hours. The kids couldn't stay alone that long.

She tried to think of who she could call for help. Her mother might be home, but she couldn't be sure. And her father's secretary could never get him on the phone quickly.

"Let me call a baby-sitter in the neighborhood to come over," she said as they passed Mick's closed door the top of the stairs. "If the kids wake up and I'm gone, they won't know what to do."

"No," he said. "We don't have time."

"But I'll use the portable phone," she said. "I can call while we're walking around."

The man paused. "Okay," he said.

They stepped into her and Mike's bedroom and Tane saw herself and the man with the gun in the mirror. He didn't look so scary from across the room. He was only a few inches taller than Tane, and he wore shorts and white tube socks with yellow stripes up around his knees. His white legs looked almost nerdy. Tane thought if he didn't have the gun she could take him.

"Hey, don't look in the mirror," the man said, ducking down as Tane picked the phone from the bedside table. She turned away from him as she dialed. She thought of calling Mike, but his Buford office was a forty-minute drive away, or 911, but how fast would they come? She dialed her mother's number. Please answer, she thought as the phone rang and rang. Please answer. But her mother never did. Tears clouded her vision and her legs weakened as her plan dissolved.

"She's not home," she said, pushing the off button.

"Come on," the man said. "Hurry and let's get out of here."

Holding onto the phone, she opened a drawer and pulled out a pair of shorts and a shirt.

"Let's go," the man said.

"Wait, I need shoes." She knelt at the closet and picked up a pair of white slip-on Ked's and stuck them under her arm, never letting go of the phone.

"I'm going to try to call the baby-sitter one more time," she said as they went back down the stairs.

"No," the man said.

"It'll just take a second," she pleaded.

The man stopped halfway down the stairs. "Okay," he said, "but make it quick."

Tane dialed her father's office.

"Milton's Foods," the receptionist said.

"This is Tane. I need my dad now," she said.

At that moment she heard her father say, "Tane?"

"Daddy, there's a man kidnapping me," she said as the man grabbed her arm with a latex gloved hand that pinched her skin. "Come get my kids."

Tane wasn't sure her father had heard the last part because the man jerked the phone from her and pressed the off button. He reacted so slowly, Tane thought she might just run out the door if the kids hadn't been in the house.

"That was so stupid," he said. "Now we really have to hurry before the police get here."

He pushed her through the den and out the garage door as he tossed the phone toward her big chair.

"Here," he said, pulling a black satin blindfold from his back pocket. "Wear this."

Tane held her clothes and shoes under her arm and pulled the blindfold over her head. It was the kind flight attendants hand out for overseas trips, except this one was much nicer than those throwaway versions. It was from Victoria's Secret.

✢ ✢ ✢

An occasional switchboard malfunction at Milton's Institutional Foods simultaneously rang Milton's and his receptionist's telephones. Milton was meeting with his brother, Tim, when he picked up the phone and heard his daughter's quavering voice.

"Tane?" he said.

When she said a man was kidnapping her, he stood and said, "What? Is he there now? We're on our way!" But the line was dead.

"That was Tane," he said as he slammed down the phone.

"She was real upset and crying and said there's a man there to kidnap her and the kids. Let's go!"

Milton and Tim ran through the front office toward the door.

"Robin, call the law!" Milton yelled at the receptionist. "Get them over to Tane's house. Somebody's kidnapping her."

They jumped into Tim's maroon Jeep Cherokee and headed across town.

✝ ✝ ✝

The glove pinched Tane's arm again as the man guided her through the garage.

"Wait," she said. "Let me lock the door so the kids will be okay."

"I'll do it," the man said. Tane stood in the middle of her garage, her bare feet on the cool cement, as he went back to lock the door. Run, she thought. Throw off this blindfold and run to a neighbor's house and call the police. But she couldn't think who would be home this time of day. Dot across the street started working when Lou died, and nobody was home during the day next door. Plus, running meant leaving the man with the mask and the gun alone with Kaylan and Mick. He might take one of them. She couldn't risk that. She stood frozen in the middle of her garage.

"Okay," the man said, taking her arm again. "Let's go."

The blindfold did not fit snugly all the way around her eyes, so Tane could see the ground below her as he led her to the passenger side of an old maroon and white sedan, which was backed into the driveway behind her Jeep. He dropped her arm and opened the door. "Get in," he said.

Tane lifted her right hand in front of her to find the top of the open door and steady herself. She could see the seat, but she didn't want to step into the car with her left foot first as she normally would. If she did, the man would know she could see. So she turned her back to the seat and eased down onto it as she held the door with her right hand and her clothes under her left arm. She swung her feet in and put them on the grimy carpet. The cracked vinyl scratched the backs of her legs. When the man closed the door she automatically reached for the seat belt. What a stupid idea, she thought, pulling her hand back. She spread her clothes on her lap to cover her legs, and put her shoes on top.

The man got in and started the engine. The car smelled stale and the air inside was thick, like a window had been left open in the rain and the car had been parked in the sun to dry. Her window was rolled down halfway. The man didn't turn on the air conditioner. Tane wondered if he was still wearing his stocking hat. A guy driving a smelly old car like this one might not be smart enough to take off his mask driving down the street. Maybe the police would see him and get suspicious.

"Can you see?" he asked. His voice sounded more clear than before. The mask must be off.

"No," she said.

"Put your head down," he said.

Tane leaned down toward the middle of the front seat as the man shifted the car into gear. She could see the revolver held tightly in the waistband of his shorts. In fact, she could have reached out and grabbed the black handle, but she wasn't sure she could pull it away without a fight.

Images of Kaylan and Mick flashed in her mind. What would they do when they woke up? Kaylan might walk out the front door looking for her. She needed to get back to them. She rocked toward the door as the car turned left out of her driveway, and again when it turned left out of the subdivision. In a minute they would be at the traffic light at Thompson Bridge Road. A hot breeze swirled through the car. The man's window must have been open too. Tane turned her chin a little more so she could look under her blindfold and see out her window. No trees or signs rose into her tiny horizontal field of view. They must be passing the cemetery, approaching Thompson Bridge. She inched her shoulder up slightly from her slumped position and slid closer to the door.

The car slowed down and began to turn left onto Thompson Bridge, and she rose up, stuck out her hand and waved.

"What are you doing!" the man shouted. The car lurched as he grabbed her shoulder and pushed her down.

"I don't know," Tane said, jerking her arm back in.

"I've got a gun, you know, and I don't want to have to use it."

Tane closed her eyes, pulled both arms underneath her and curled into a tight little ball. She tried to keep from crying, but could not. All of her strength would not steady her heaving shoulders as she sobbed. She was too afraid to do anything to save herself. She couldn't grab the gun. She couldn't call for help. She couldn't open the door and jump out. So she cried. Her shoulders heaved and tears soaked the bottom edge of the blindfold. She tried to calm herself by taking deep breaths. The stale, thick air made her stomach turn.

"I think I'm going to be sick," she said.

"Throw up in the floor," the man responded.

She thought she would, and she knew she would feel better if she did. But it wouldn't come. Even when she pulled hard on her stomach muscles and exhaled from her diaphragm it wouldn't come.

"Can't I sit up?" she asked. "I can't breathe down here."

"No," he said.

The hot wind made the straps of her tank top flap softly against her shoulders. She had to get some of that air. She had to take the risk. She rose up slightly and breathed. The man didn't say anything. She rose up a little more and breathed again. Her head was still lower than the dashboard, but the move settled her stomach slightly. She opened her eyes and peeked under her mask to see a Kangaroo store sign, the one right across from Gold's. She was just here a few of hours ago with Kaylan and Mick. Was anybody she knew out in the parking lot looking toward the street, toward this car with her in it?

Riding through Gainesville, Tane recognized each turn

the car made and saw enough through the space below her blindfold to know exactly where she was. She saw the steeple of the First Baptist Church as the man drove toward downtown. Later, as traffic slowed, she saw the sign at Morgan Cleaners, where she took her clothes. I know people in there, she thought. Maybe they can help me. But before she gathered the courage to unlock the door and open it, the car was half a block away. As they rolled slowly past the fire station Tane again thought of jumping out. What if he shoots me in the back, she thought. She saw her body sprawled on the sidewalk, blood spilling from her as a crowd gathered. She didn't move.

✟ ✟ ✟

Alecia Schact sat in her class at North Georgia College in Dahlonega thinking of other ways to spend a summer afternoon. I'll go see Tane, she thought. Alecia and Tane had been friends since seventh grade and they still got together once or twice a month. The Shannons' house was a mile off the highway on Alecia's way home, so it would be easy to drop by. She drove south toward Gainesville after class, looking forward to laughing with Tane and watching the kids play.

When she got to the house she parked behind Tane's red Jeep and walked through the garage to the door. She knocked on the window. Tane didn't come, so she tried the knob. Locked. Strange, she thought. Tane never locks the door when she's at home.

"Tane!" she yelled as she knocked again. No response. Concerned now, she walked quickly out of the garage and around to the front door, which she found unlocked.

"Tane?" she said, stepping inside. "You home?"

She stood and listened. A television was on in the den so she started toward it. Then she heard Mick cry upstairs and she turned to go up. Tane must be with him.

"Tane?" she said as she climbed the stairs. "You up here?"

No response. Her stomach began to knot as the terrible possibilities flashed in her mind and Mick's cries grew louder.

At the top of the stairs his door was closed. She turned the knob and pushed. Mick stood in his crib screaming and Alecia went to him and lifted him out.

"It's okay, Mick," she said softly as she cradled him on her shoulder and stroked the back of his head. "Everything's okay."

Several minutes had passed since she arrived. Tane would never have left Mick in the house alone, even for a moment. She glanced into Tane's and Mike's empty bedroom then went downstairs. Mick settled as they walked. In the den she found Kaylan sleeping on the sofa and "The Guiding Light" on the television. She knew Kaylan would panic if she woke up and her mother was gone, so she left her.

Looking for clues in the living room, she tried to think of what to do or who to call. A yellow pickup truck drove back and forth several times in front of the house. She walked to the front door and the man driving stopped and rolled down his window as she stepped outside.

"Is everything all right?" he asked.

"I think so," she said, surprised by the question and not ready to tell a stranger that something was terribly wrong.

He stepped out and walked toward the door. Alecia turned slightly so that her shoulder was between him and Mick.

"I live around the corner," he said. "My brother works with Milton. His office called and asked me to come over and see if everything was okay."

"I don't know," Alecia said. "I'm looking for Tane. I don't know where she is."

As she spoke a tan sheriff's department car squealed around the corner and stopped in front of the house. Alecia squeezed Mick to keep herself from shaking.

✝ ✝ ✝

Billy, Mike's ten-year-old patient, gripped the arms of the big chair tightly and said, "L E F O D P L T."

"That's good," Mike said. "Now read the next line."

As Billy read, Mike heard the door open behind him and saw light fill the room. He hated to be interrupted during an eye examination.

"Excuse me, Dr. Shannon," said Jan, Mike's assistant. "Robin, in Milton's office, needs to talk to you on the phone."

"Ask her if I can call her back," Mike said.

"She says it's an emergency."

"I'm sorry," Mike said to Billy and his mother. "Please excuse me a minute." He walked quickly down the hall to his office, squinting slightly as he adjusted to the light, and answered the phone without sitting at his desk.

"Hello, this is Mike," he said.

"Mike, this is Robin. Do you know if Tane was going over to the new house today?"

Strange question, he thought. He quickly recounted morning conversations. "I don't think so," he said. "She didn't mention it. Why?"

"Well, she called her dad and said she's being kidnapped."

"She what?" Mike said, putting his right hand on the desk for support.

"Tane called Milton a minute ago and said she's being kidnapped," she repeated.

"Where? How?" Mike asked.

"I don't know," Jan said. "Milton's going to the house right now."

"Has anybody called the police?" Mike asked.

"Yes, and they're on their way."

"I'm going there, too," Mike said. "I'll get there as fast as I can. Bye."

He hung up the phone and continued to grip it, leaning heavily on the desk. Words and images swirled in his head without coming together as clear thoughts. He tried to make a mental list of what to do as he walked to the front desk. He had seen things like this happen on TV. What did they do? Car keys. He reached into his pocket and found them. Anything else?

"Are you all right?" asked Cheryl, his other assistant.

Mike was cold — shivering — like he had jumped into an icy lake. He turned back toward his office, then turned again toward the front door.

"I don't know," he said, turning and turning again. "Tane called Milton and said she's being kidnapped."

"Oh my God," Cheryl said.

"Tane's been kidnapped," Mike whispered. "Tane's been kidnapped."

"I have to go," he told Jan and Cheryl. He broke out of his circular pacing and walked back to the examination room.

"I'm sorry I can't finish this eye exam," he said. "I have a personal emergency. I'm sorry. I have to leave right now."

Mike reached for his keys again and made a straight line to the front door. As soon as it shut behind him, he ran to his car. He got in and squealed the tires backing out of his parking space. A red light stopped him just before he reached the interstate, giving him time to find the emergency flasher switch. He accelerated down the entrance ramp and watched the speedometer needle rise past one hundred. He would cut the usual forty-minute drive time in half.

✝ ✝ ✝

Two police cars were parked in front of the house when Milton and his brother drove up. Milton jumped out and ran to the open front door, where Alecia stood holding Mick in one arm while her other arm wrapped around the shoulders of a sleepy, confused Kaylan.

"What's going on?" Milton asked. "Where's the law?"

"Inside," Alecia said. "I don't know what's going on."

Officer Dale Long came to the door and told Milton that only Kaylan and Mick had been in the house when he arrived. The two men stepped inside, away from the children, before Milton told the officer about Tane's call.

"I think you need to get the kids out of here," Long said. "We'll have people all over the place soon."

Milton agreed and asked Alecia to take them to her house until they could straighten things out. Tim was standing at the door by then, and two more patrol cars had driven up.

"What do you think?" Tim asked.

"I think I'd better call the bank before they close," Milton said. "If somebody has Tane it's got to be for money."

He went to Tim's Jeep and called Will White at the First National Bank. He didn't know how much he would need, but he expected it would be a lot.

✝ ✝ ✝

The man turned the car right and drove toward the interstate. Before he got there he turned into the parking lot behind Burger King and stopped the car.

"What are we doing?" Tane asked

"I'll come around for you," he said opening his door.

"You mean we're getting out here?" Tane asked.

"We're switching cars," the man said.

He opened Tane's door and said, "Bring your clothes." She stepped barefoot onto the blistering parking lot, and he took her arm as if he were escorting a date. The glove was still there. Tane heard children playing nearby.

"Don't I look funny wearing this blindfold?" she asked.

"Don't worry," the man said. "Nobody can see us. Just act real casual."

She thought about jerking her arm away and running toward Burger King, but that gun.

The man opened the door of a charcoal gray Firebird Trans Am and said, "Get in."

The leather bucket seat burned her legs. She gritted her teeth and inhaled sharply. The man shut the door and walked around while she spread her clothes on her lap again. She was confused and mad. What does he want to kidnap me for, she thought. If he can afford a car like this, he must have money.

The man got in, started the car and turned on the air conditioner. As he reached over to lock Tane's door, she tipped her head back slightly and saw his face — the mask was gone — less than a foot away. She studied its details. A soft face. Not fat, but soft. Silver and black stubble emerging from powdery white skin, wiry black hair growing just over his ears and messed up from wearing that sock hat. Aviator-style wire-rim glasses and a short neck.

"Get your head down," he said.

Did he see me looking at him, Tane wondered. He'll kill me for sure if he knows I saw him. She leaned toward the console as the man drove through an intersection and onto the ramp to the interstate.

"You can sit up now," he said. "Nobody will notice you out here."

She rose up and leaned her head back against the head-rest. Neither of them spoke as the man drove south toward Atlanta. Alternating fears raced wildly in Tane's head. Would he kill her? Rape her? Would she ever see her family again? She replayed her words to her father in her head. She hoped he had understood her plea and somebody was at the house with the kids by now.

The man left the expressway at the Flowery Branch exit and turned right, toward Tane's mother's house. A few minutes later he turned back toward Gainesville on McEver Road. If he was driving around in circles to confuse her, it wasn't working. Tane would have known where she was even if the blindfold had worked. She didn't realize, however, that the man had gone ten miles out of his way so he could drive down a road that bore his own last name, Radford Road.

When he turned left onto Browns Bridge Road, they were within a block of Mama Dese's house. I wonder if she knows yet, Tane thought.

"Why are you doing this?" she asked.

"I need the money," he said.

"This is a nice car," she said. "You must have money somewhere."

"Yeah, right," he said. "You just don't understand. You've got it made. You've always had it made with your rich daddy and all. Well, I deserve some too, and I intend to get it."

Tane said nothing for a moment.

Then she asked, "What do you think you deserve?"

"Half a million."

The car crossed a green metal bridge over Lake Lanier into Forsyth County and Tane lost her bearings. She thought they must be headed toward Highway 400 to go the mountains, but she wasn't sure.

"Can we call my house now to make sure somebody is there with my kids?" she asked.

"No," the man said.

"But Daddy might not have understood me," she said.

"You shouldn't have called him anyway," he said. "We'll call soon enough."

Tane began to cry again. She pictured Kaylan and Mick's little faces, laughing as they played on the living room floor with Mike. She saw Mike pulling them around the driveway in a red wagon. She wasn't in either picture.

She swayed and pitched as the car took sharp turns, and she realized she had to use the bathroom. We must be in the mountains, she thought.

"Do you feel lost?" the man asked.

"What?" she said.

"Do you feel lost? Do you have any idea where you're at?"

"No. How could I? No."

"Good."

The car turned sharply, slowed and stopped. Tane looked out the corners of her blindfold and saw a phone booth. Thinking that the man was calling to get money, that this might be the beginning of the end of her ordeal, she breathed deeply. She caught herself before she exhaled a "whew." He might hear it and figure out she could see.

"What are you doing?" she asked.

"I'm calling," he said, covering the gun with his shirttail and stepping out of the car. "Put your head down."

"I need to go to the bathroom," she said.

"Not here," he said. "We'll be there soon. Put your head down."

"Ask about the kids," she said as he got out of the car.

Tane ducked but kept her head high enough to peek around from underneath her blindfold. She saw a customer at the gas pump about thirty feet away and thought about hollering or running toward him. Her kidnapper turned his back to the car briefly as he put a quarter in the phone and punched a number.

Go now! she thought. But her body froze. Just like in front of the fire station, she saw herself lying dead on the parking lot. This time she felt the bullet in her back.

✝ ✝ ✝

Kathy Sheffield never expected to be a crime scene technician. She was a sheriff's department secretary — one who took meticulous notes and typed a hundred twenty words a minute. Her boss, Captain Ron Attaway, suggested that her close attention to detail made her an ideal candidate for crime scene technician, and she thought the job sounded exciting. Now, after months of training and a year in her new position, Kathy found herself driving to the home of a childhood friend who had disappeared mysteriously and was reported kidnapped. The clues she found might bring Tane home alive.

Kathy and Tane had drifted apart over the years. In junior high and high school they found different interests, different friends. In fact, Kathy hadn't recognized Tane's married name when she received the initial kidnapping report. Only when she was driving to the Shannons' house, when the radio dispatcher said this was Milton Robson's daughter, did Kathy's emotions become involved in the case.

Tane Robson. Kathy and her parents had camped with Tane and her parents near the lake twenty years ago. They had ridden horses together. Kathy must have been seven or eight. Tane was two years younger and so tiny riding that light colored Shetland pony — what was her name, Misty? — beside her parents high up on their bays. It had been too long since Kathy had been on a horse.

Only once since Kathy became a technician had she

handled the case of a friend. Just like this time, she hadn't recognized Ann's married name until she arrived at the scene — the deep woods where Ann had killed herself. She hoped that Tane had just run away — that she hadn't been kidnapped and her life wasn't in danger.

Officers Dale Long and Art Jetton, after looking around the house, reported no signs of a struggle. Kathy slipped on two pairs of latex gloves — sweat might soak through one pair on a hot day and leave fingerprints — grabbed her camera and went in through the garage door, which Long had left open. For the first few minutes she was alone in the house, looking for evidence of contact between Tane and an intruder.

Kathy noted that Tane had been in the den last. For one thing, the television was on. A pile of clothes sat partially folded beside a lounge chair, and on the floor between the chair and a rocking horse was a mug of coffee. She took a picture. On the sofa lay a cordless telephone. Unusual. Another picture. She heard other cars drive up, and looked out the door to see Captain Judy Mecum, Lieutenant John Attaway, who would take charge of the investigation, and investigators David Gazaway and Marty Nix. Kathy met them in the garage and filled them in. They joined her in her search for evidence.

As they entered the house, Sheriff Mecum arrived.

✝ ✝ ✝

Dick Mecum rarely took over an investigation. He'd hired good people to do that. Instead, he observed with dark, serious eyes from the periphery, and made mental notes as his investigators collected evidence and shared theories.

He also prayed. For the Hall County sheriff, prayer was as important to finding answers as evidence was. Before going to work every morning, he spent at least an hour reading the Bible, memorizing scriptures, preparing for the following week's Sunday School lesson, then offering specific cases to God and asking for guidance. At work, when faced with an especially difficult case, he sometimes called several deputies into his office, closed the door and prayed with them for guidance. Then throughout each day he would recall the words of the apostle Paul, "Pray in the Spirit on all occasions with all kinds of prayers and requests."

At the Shannon home the sheriff stood with one foot up on the threshold between the garage and the den, silently scanning the room for clues about Tane — family photographs, toys, anything — while watching his detectives. Then for a moment he allowed his eyes to glaze over, focusing on nothing, praying, "Show me something, Lord. What do You want me to do here?" He tried to clear his mind of all distractions, but he couldn't shake the thought, get help. Don't work this one alone. He finally laid the thought aside and asked God to watch over Tane, to bring her home safe and unharmed. He asked Him also to comfort her family and to protect her children.

All this he did with his eyes open. To the detectives, who knew something of the sheriff's conviction but not of his longing for constant fellowship with God, he appeared merely to be in deep thought.

"Thy will be done," he prayed, his tongue forming the words inside his mouth and his lips moving almost visibly. The prayer frightened him, for God's will often differed from his own. Crime victims too often were not kept safe and criminals sometimes went free. To reassure himself that God heard his prayer and was participating actively with him, Mecum meditated briefly on Jeremiah 29:12, "You will call upon me and come and pray to me and I will listen."

The strong feeling returned to him, get help. This was God communicating, telling him to bring in more resources: the FBI, the Georgia Bureau of Investigation. The message came so clearly it buoyed him. God was right there, feeding him answers, ordaining him to take this case to its conclusion — to bring Tane home.

Focusing again on the job at hand, he watched as Kathy knelt by a table with a telephone on it just inside the door. She touched nothing in this first stage of the investigation.

She just looked, made notes and took pictures. She pointed a small light across the surface of the table and squinted to see any fingerprints. Beside the telephone lay two plastic bags taped shut, each with a sheet of yellow paper inside. The sheriff leaned over for a closer look. The paper appeared to have writing on the side facing down. Kathy had already noted the unusual bags, suspecting they might be a ransom note. She couldn't touch them yet, not until she had photographed them.

She held her camera to photograph the table just as the phone rang. She flinched, startled. She and the investigators all looked toward the sheriff. He nodded to Kathy then put his arms together and spread them slowly, the way a director would quiet a choir. Kathy picked up the receiver with a double-gloved finger and thumb.

"Hello," she said.

"Who is this?" a man's voice asked. Kathy heard highway noise in the background as if the call were coming from a pay phone. This could be the one.

"This is Kathy," she said.

"Whose residence is this?" he asked.

"Tane's."

"Did you find my note?" She looked at the sheriff and nodded. This was their man.

"You left a note?" she asked. She waited for him to answer, but he didn't. She listened to the background noise, straining to hear anything that would tell her where he was. "Where?"

"By the phone. Is the police there?" the man said.

"No," Kathy said. She glanced down at the plastic bag with the paper. She tried to stall him, to pick up any clue. "Can you hold till I find it?"

"No," he said. "It's by the phone."

"Which phone? Which phone? There are several in the house."

"It's by the telephone," he said and he hung up.

"That's him," Kathy said as she replaced the receiver. "It's a real one."

She took two quick photographs of the table, then picked up the plastic bag by a corner and turned it over. "And here's his note."

The red letters were large and shaky, barely legible. The first page read, "I have your wife. NO COPS. NO FBI. Only you can get her back." Page two read, "500,000 in used bills only. 5, 10, 20. She will not be harmed. I will call."

"Okay," Mecum said calmly. "We know what we have here. We're going to bring Tane Shannon home safe and unharmed."

Kathy's eyes betrayed her surprise at the statement. Rarely did the sheriff make such bold pronouncements. The words came out before he had considered them and they startled even him. He almost said out loud, "Did I say that?"

God had put the words in his mouth, the way He did sometimes when he prayed. Without question, God was with him, beside him in the doorway. He was in charge of this investigation and He would bring Tane home safe and unharmed. The sheriff only had to follow His lead.

✝ ✝ ✝

The man got back in the car.

"You can sit up now," he said as he drove away from the filling station. "Are you sure you can't see?"

"No," she said. "Did you talk to somebody?"

"Your mother," he said.

"Are my kids all right?" she asked.

"I didn't ask, but I'm sure they are," he said.

Tane relaxed momentarily. Her mother was with Kaylan and Mick and her father must be somewhere trying to get the money the man wanted. If all went well, she would ride around a little while longer, the man would get his money and let her go, and she would be home by bedtime.

Twelve

From the violent man you rescued me.
— Psalm 18:48

August 10, 1992
3:30 p.m.

Holding the vibrating steering wheel tightly with both hands, Mike glanced down at his car phone and thought he should call somebody. If he could say it out loud to somebody — Tane's been kidnapped — they would both realize how absurd it was, how Mike's imagination had run away with him. Then he could go back and finish Billy's examination and hope people didn't say how crazy he was. But who could he call? When big things happened he always called Tane. He was afraid to call home, afraid she wouldn't answer. He concentrated on the road.

Half a mile ahead a car pulled into the left lane to pass a truck. Mike eased back on the accelerator and looked down the highway beyond the passing car. All clear, he sped up again and guided his Maxima into the emergency lane, taking care not to swerve too sharply and lose control. He resisted the urge to look at the driver as he passed. He wanted to apologize for driving so crazy. As soon as he returned to the highway, he looked in the mirror to make sure everybody behind him was all right. Mike looked back often expecting to see blue lights and determined that if they came, they would have to follow him all the way home.

He left the interstate at Exit 6 and turned left, speeding through the intersection by the Burger King. He slowed down through town, fearing he might hit another car or somebody crossing the street, and accelerated again when he reached Thompson Bridge Road. His tires squealed when he turned right onto Mount Vernon and again when he turned into the subdivision. Around the curve and down the hill he saw the house. Yellow crime scene tape circled the perimeter of the yard and blocked the driveway. *Oh, God, is she inside? Is she dead? Why else would they put up that yellow tape?*

Police cars lined both sides of the street. He slammed on the brakes behind one of them and scrambled out, his emergency lights still flashing. Spotting the closest policeman, he ran to him. Tane's brother, Todd, intercepted him, followed closely by Milton.

"What's going on?" Mike asked. "Is Tane all right?"

"She's going to be okay," Todd said. "It'll be all right."

"So is it true?" Mike asked. "Did somebody kidnap her? Where are the kids?"

"The kids are okay," Milton said. "Alecia came over and they're with her. Ed's going to take them to his house. Apparently this guy just wants money and he says he isn't going to hurt Tane. We'll get the money. We'll get her back."

Milton sounded confident. Mike looked over his father-in-law's shoulder and saw Tane's mother crying, dashing any reassurance he might have felt. A man in a suit walked toward him. "Dr. Shannon?" he asked.

"Yes," Mike said.

"I'm Eddie Reeves from the Sheriff's Department. Can we talk with you a minute over here?"

"Yes, please," Mike answered, following him to a tan sheriff's department car.

Mike asked the first question. "So what happened here? What happened to my wife?"

"Apparently your wife has been kidnapped," Reeves said. "We found a note demanding money — five hundred thousand dollars. That's all we know right now. I'm afraid we have to ask you some difficult questions."

"Just get her back," Mike said.

"That's our plan," Reeves said. "Now have y'all had any problems, marital problems, in the last year or so?"

"No."

"None whatsoever?"

"No."

"Has there been anybody showing interest in Tane that you know of?"

"If there was, I didn't know about it."

"Has there been anybody that you've had a problem with that may be wanting to get back at you for some reason?"

"Not that I know. I have good relationships with all my patients. If anybody was this mad, I'd give them a refund."

Mike listened to himself answer the questions. His body, even his mouth, was working automatically while his mind focused on Tane. Where was she? Who had her? Were they hurting her? Raping her? Was she still alive?

"Okay. If you would, just keep mulling over in your mind anything, even if it's minute," Reeves said.

"I can't think of anything. Except, this guy that played at Milton's party on Saturday night, Jason somebody. He's a Nashville singer, country music singer. He kept leering at her from the word go. I figured that's part of the act. You know, look at all the women and flirt with them and stuff."

Now focusing on Reeves, Mike said, "Do you know anything yet? Do you have any clues?"

"All we know so far is that your wife called her father and said she was being kidnapped. We came here and found a note demanding money. That's it. So if there's anything else you can think of …"

"If I could …" Mike interrupted.

"I know, I know, you've probably got a million things on your mind."

"If there's anything … I just want y'all to find her. I mean, we're happy. We're moving into a new house. Finally, I'll be ten minutes from work. Finally, one week away from moving, I get a phone call that says Tane's been kidnapped. You tell me what to do."

"You just let us do our job," Reeves said.

"Would it help if I looked around inside?" Mike asked.

"Not yet," the investigator said turning away. "When

we finish our preliminary investigation you can go in."

Mike walked toward Tane's mother. She had stopped crying. He hugged her and she started again. "Oh, Mike, what are we going to do?" she asked. Mike didn't answer.

Brenda didn't know where Tane got her strength. It certainly wasn't from her. Brenda cried easily. She worried daily about her parents, her children, her grandchildren, everybody. Every morning she called Tane to see that she and Mike and the kids were all right, just as Dese still called her every morning.

Brenda had just finished the flower arrangement for Mike's office when the call came. The telephone trembled against her face and ear when she learned somebody had taken Tane.

She drove straight over, concentrating on driving slowly and carefully. She wanted all the police looking for Tane, not seeing about her in a wreck.

Todd ran to Brenda when she parked the car at the curb. The police were making everybody stay outside. Milton was back outside, too, talking with a deputy. Brenda eased over toward the two men so she could hear better. With a wave of his hand the deputy shooed her away.

She didn't say, "But I'm her mother," though she wished she had. She stayed out of the way instead.

Mike drove up a moment later and he came to her. Brenda stepped away from him and they looked toward the front of the house. Kaylan's plastic pool sat in the yard. Kaylan was such a mama's girl. She clung to Tane's leg whenever she met a stranger. What would she do without her mother — even for a day or two? And what if Tane didn't come home?

✝ ✝ ✝

"Put on your shoes," the man said. "We'll be there soon."

"Be where?" Tane asked.

"Never mind that," he said. "Just put your shoes on."

Tane didn't know how long they had been driving when the man turned left off the highway onto a one-lane road. Or was it a driveway? The bumpy lane dropped quickly as it wound away from the highway, cutting a narrow path through a hardwood forest. They seemed to have traveled about a mile into the woods when the man steered the car off the road and turned off the engine.

"Stay there," he said. "I'll get your door."

She glanced around quickly from underneath her blindfold as the man walked around the car. A long, white and sulfur colored mobile home, which she assumed was their destination, sat directly in front of the car. About twenty yards to the left was a low cinder-block building painted the color of the tan earth around it. It had a tin roof. She thought the man might live there or have a partner waiting inside. He interrupted her speculation by opening her door, then he took her arm with a warm, damp hand — the gloves were gone — and led her toward a wooden stoop. A loose brick lay on the ground in front of the steps, and Tane knew she wasn't supposed to see it. Instead of stepping over it, she kicked it with her right foot and stumbled.

"It's okay," the man said, tightening his grip on her arm. "I got you. You're about to go up two steps to the door."

When they reached the stoop, he opened the metal door and guided her inside.

Tane had lived in a trailer before. Her grandparents owned a trailer park and Tane's family had lived there for awhile when she was in the second grade. She liked to run down the long hall banging on the paneled walls, and she liked the little bitty rooms because they were cozy. She recognized the burnt orange shag carpet and the smell of mildew and wood paneling. But they didn't remind her of home.

"Go left," the man said.

She turned down the hallway that she knew would lead to bedrooms. She also remembered they would pass a bathroom along the way.

"I have to go to the bathroom," she said.

"Okay," the man said.

She put her right hand on the wall and found her way down the hallway. The man still held her left arm. In her left hand she held her extra clothes. She saw the bathroom door and caught herself short before stepping inside.

"Is this the bathroom?" she asked.

"How did you know that?"

"I felt you stop here and assumed this was it," she said.

"Oh, okay," he said. "Well, this is it."

He guided her through a small alcove with a washer and dryer to the bathroom door.

"Put your extra clothes right here," he said, patting the top of the washer.

She did and then stepped inside the bathroom and waited for him to close the door. He didn't. She put her hand on the sink and felt her way to the toilet. She stood over it and waited another moment. Still, the door remained open. She couldn't see if he had moved or turned away until she pulled down her shorts and sat down. The white tennis shoes and tube socks were still there. Her stomach turned. He was watching her and she couldn't stop him. She couldn't even tell him she knew he was watching. She forced herself to finish quickly, then pulled up her shorts then felt her way out of the bathroom.

"Go left," the man said. She put her hand against the wall again and made her way down the hall. He took her left elbow; she flinched. She hated his touch. They came to a door directly in front of her that led into a bedroom at the end of the trailer. She lifted her chin slightly and saw a spool bed with a pink and white striped sheet over it. A rectangle of filtered sunlight lay on the carpet beside the bed. With no other lights turned on and no apparent attempt to decorate, the room appeared gray and bleak.

The man led Tane to the bed. "You might as well get comfortable," he said. "We're going to be here awhile."

Tane didn't understand. She still thought this was a one-day thing.

"What do you mean?" she said. "Aren't you going to

call my family? Can't you get the money and let me go?"

"Banks are closed," he said. "Your father won't be able to get the money until tomorrow morning."

"He can get it," she said. "They'll open it up for him. If you call him they can work something out."

"I didn't know that," the man said.

"Well, I'm telling you now," she said. "So go call him."

"That wasn't my plan," he said, "and I don't want to change it and take any more chances. So you might as well get comfortable. The banks open at eight-thirty tomorrow morning. I'll do it then."

"But you could finish everything tonight and not have to worry about it tomorrow," Tane said.

"Tomorrow," he said. "I'll do it tomorrow. Now you just settle down. You can have the bed to yourself. I'll stay over here on the chair."

Tane sat at the edge of the bed let it all sink in. The mask, the gun, the car, the drive, the woods. Now she was going to spend the night in this place. With this man. The air in the room was hot and thick like the inside of the man's first car. For the first time she realized she might not go home again. Something in his plan would go wrong and he would have to shoot her or burn the trailer with her in it. He wouldn't want to take a chance of leaving her alive. Lisa, Todd's wife, had told her about a TV movie she saw where a kidnapped woman was burned up in a house, and another one about woman who was kidnapped and brainwashed and made a sex slave. Which movie has this guy seen, she wondered.

"Do you want something to eat?" he said. "A Little Debbie or some juice?"

Probably drugged or poisoned, she thought.

"No," she said.

He must have sensed her fear. "I haven't done anything to it. The Little Debbies are still in the package."

"No."

"Well you might as well take off your shoes and get comfortable."

The man opened the window and turned on a ceiling fan, drawing in cool, fresh air. Tane realized they were in the mountains. She pulled off her shoes and curled up tightly on her side, turning her back to the man. She felt his eyes on her, the way she had felt them when she was in the bathroom, eyeing her; waiting. The mattress smelled musty and it sank in the middle, pulling her down into it. She tried to block out thoughts of him watching her by listening to the quiet, straining her ears for any hopeful sign — a car, a plane, anything that would tell her she wasn't alone in the middle of nowhere. Only the occasional caw of a distant crow broke the silence.

"I'm going to the bathroom," the man said. "Don't move and don't try to scream."

When she heard him walking down the hall, Tane rolled over onto her back so she could see around the room from underneath her blindfold. She was afraid to take it off, in case he looked back. A night stand beside the bed held a clock radio that faced away from her. A dresser with a brand new white fitted sheet draped over the mirror sat against the wall across the room. A wooden chair sat beside the bed. She looked carefully at the window and decided it was big enough for her to fit through if she got a chance to escape. She would run straight into the woods and hide. The toilet flushed and Tane rolled back onto her side again and curled up. The man came back into the room and sat in the chair, and a wave of nausea swept through her.

She wasn't getting out of here alive. "Oh, God," she prayed silently, "if he's going to kill me anyway, just get it over fast. Let him put that gun to my head and shoot me."

At the moment she prayed her blood ran ice cold. If she died tonight she might go to hell. Never had she seriously considered the possibility, but now it lay clearly before her — the fiery, eternal suffering of hell. She had been saved when she was seven years old back at Poplar Springs Baptist Church. She could still feel the warm water around her. She had always been told: Once saved, always saved. But now that she was facing death, she no longer was so sure. And what if, years from now, Kaylan and Mick died and went to Heaven and asked, "Where's Mommy?" She might not be there.

It struck her hard. She had to escape. Not from the man, but from eternal damnation.

✝ ✝ ✝

Dese usually fixed a light supper on Monday nights after the big family lunch. She was working in the kitchen when the phone rang.

"Dese, are you all right?" It was Todd. He sounded like he was on a car phone, or maybe outside somewhere.

"Yes, I'm fine."

"Are you sure?" he asked. He wasn't ready to come out and say it.

"Yes, honey," Dese insisted. "What's wrong?"

"Tane's …" He coughed and couldn't finish the sentence. Dese braced herself for bad news. Todd took a deep breath and tried again. "Tane's been kidnapped."

Dese slammed her hand hard on the bar and cried, "No! She can't be! That's my baby!"

"I know, she's my sister, too," Todd said, still choking. "But she has."

For nearly a minute neither of them could speak. They each held a telephone receiver and cried, Dese standing in her kitchen, Todd sitting in his mother's car in the street in front of his sister's house. Finally Dese asked, "When did it happen?"

Todd told her the little bit he knew and explained that the police weren't letting anybody inside the house. He would have to call her with more information when he got it.

"How is Brenda?" Dese asked.

"She's okay," Todd said, but he knew she wasn't. She had asked Todd to call her mother because she never would get the words out.

As soon as Dese hung up she called her sister Pat, who lived twenty miles away. "I'll be there in a little bit," Pat said.

Then Pat went straight to the bathroom, which she called her holy room, where she kept her Bible and did most of her serious praying. She closed the door and said, "Please, Lord, give us Your word. Give me a word just for Tane." Then she opened her Bible in the middle and began to read, and immediately it was there.

"The LORD lives! Praise be to my Rock! Exalted be God my Savior! He is the God who avenges me, who subdues nations under me, who saves me from my enemies. You exalted me above my foes; from violent men you rescued me."

"That's it!" she said out loud. "'From violent men you rescued me.' Oh, Lord, I thank You and praise You for that word."

Confident that Tane would be all right, she practically ran to her car so she could deliver the message to her sister. She didn't want to tell her over the telephone.

A dozen people were at Dese's house speaking softly or crying when Pat let herself in through the kitchen door. When she saw Dese, her eyes red and her cheeks wet, she ached to tell her what she had read. She wanted to yell to the whole house, "It's all right. I know Tane will be all right." But when she wrapped her arms around Dese, her sister's fear overwhelmed her and her tears flowed. After a moment she composed herself and said, "Dese, she's okay. Tane's okay."

"Oh, I hope so," Dese said.

"No," Pat said. "God gave me a word just for Tane. He took me straight to it. 'Thou hast delivered me from the violent man.'"

Dese lifted her eyes.

"Yes," Pat said smiling, tears still streaming. "'Thou hast delivered me from the violent man.' Psalm 18:48. He gave it to me right after we talked."

Dese tried to return the smile. "I hope you're right," she said. "I do hope you're right." They embraced again and Dese prayed silently for her own sign.

✝ ✝ ✝

Becky Bowman locked the first of three doors to the bank vault and stood alone in the change-counting room, which served as an anteroom to the most secure area of the vault. The clattering of quarters, dimes, nickels and pennies mechanically ching-chinging through the sorter now echoed in her head, even though the machine was finished and the room was as silent as a cave. She pulled open the iron-barred amber door and stepped out into the bank lobby, then pulled the door shut behind her with a loud metal clang. She swung the foot-thick stainless steel outer door smoothly on its big hinges until it clamped into place. Then she spun the dial, locking it for the night. Her phone was ringing, so she hurried around the corner to her office, which was smaller than the vault and, similarly, had no windows.

"Becky, this is Joyce. Have you locked the vault?" Becky heard urgency in her voice. Customers sometimes called with after-hours cash requests and she hated to let them down, but this time she would have to.

"I'm sorry, Joyce, I just spun the dial," she said. "Is there anything I can do to help?"

"One of our customers needs some money. Is there any way you can get back in?"

"Not until tomorrow," Becky said. "Are we talking about a lot of money? Maybe we could do something else."

"Becky," she said, "we need a lot of money."

A timer on the vault at the First National Bank of Gainesville ensured that after Becky locked it, no one, even with the combination, could enter it until seven-thirty the following morning.

"I'll call the Browns Bridge Road branch and see if they've locked their vault yet and get back with you," Becky said.

Browns Bridge was locked, too, and Becky called Joyce to tell her. Joyce sighed heavily and said, "Oh no."

Becky, who was vice president of teller operations, stepped out of her office and stood behind the teller counter when Will White, with his head down, hurried across the lobby and into Harold Westbrook's office. Harold ran the bank's main branch. A moment later Harold stepped out and asked Becky to join them. Will told her about the kidnapping and the kidnapper's demands, five hundred thousand dollars in small, used denominations.

"Do we have that in the vault?" he asked.

At almost any moment Becky, who was responsible for the vault, could provide a rough inventory from memory.

"We have about half of it here," she said, "and we can probably make up the difference from Browns Bridge."

"Milton says they don't know when this guy will call back," Will said. "It could be anytime tonight. When he calls and says, 'I want it' …"

"We can't get it, Will," Becky interrupted shakily, knowing her words might be Tane's death sentence. "There's just no way to get into the vault."

"No possible way?" Will asked.

"None. If he calls, they can let me talk to him and I'll explain that nobody can get into the vault after hours. It's physically impossible. We can get the money together as fast as possible tomorrow morning, but that's all we can do."

Harold Westbrook told Becky to do what she had to to get the money as quickly as possible. Then the three bankers, helpless, ended their meeting. Becky walked back across the lobby, aware that the blood had drained from her face, and hoped none of the tellers would stop her. She closed the door to her office and, before the phone could ring, she prayed. "Dear Lord," she said, "please be there for Tane. Help her through her trial and give her the strength to endure. Whatever is best for her, please provide it."

In the stillness of her office, she made a connection. Without seeing or knowing God's plan for Tane or her own role in it, she believed He was in control.

✝ ✝ ✝

Mike had been standing on the corner outside his house

for over an hour when he saw the photographer. Neighbors who hardly ever spoke had already stopped and asked what was going on. Now the newspaper was there. He remembered he hadn't called his parents and hoped they hadn't heard the news on the radio or television.

"I'm going to use your car phone," he told Brenda. Her car was parked right in front of the house. A camera clicked several times as he tried to explain to his mother, then to his father, what had happened.

He heard a voice behind him as he hung up the phone. "Dr. Shannon?"

"Yes," he said looking around. It was one of the investigators.

"I'm David Gazaway. Can you come inside with me and look around?"

"Yeah, sure," Mike said.

Gazaway lifted the yellow police tape for Mike and they walked down the driveway into the garage.

"Please don't touch anything," Gazaway said as they stepped through the den door. The knob had a thin film of black dust, which Mike took to be fingerprint dust. He kept his hands close to his sides.

Mike looked around the room, now a crime scene, and swallowed hard. Much of the life had left the room even before somebody took Tane. The shelves were almost bare, photographs and other memories packed in boxes in preparation for moving to the new house. More black dust lay on the table top beside the telephone and on the wall by the light switch.

"Do you see anything that looks out of place?" Gazaway asked.

"The whole house is a mess," Mike said. "It looks like a bomb hit it."

"But can you tell if anything has been moved?" Gazaway asked.

"No, not really."

"Let's look upstairs," Gazaway said.

Mike followed the investigator up the stairs and passed Mick's room, where two other men were looking around. "Let's go in here first," Gazaway said gesturing toward Mike's and Tane's bedroom. "Anything look out of place?"

Mike sat on the end of the bed and looked around at the boxes. "I'm not sure that drawer was open," he said pointing to the dresser. "And that pad on the table might not have been there, but everything else looks the same."

"Who do you think might have done this?" Gazaway asked. "Have you thought of anything?"

"I've been trying to think," Mike said, "and I can't come up with anybody."

"What kind of money do you make? Can you come up with half a million dollars?"

"I make a decent living," Mike answered, "but even if I sold everything we own I couldn't scrape up that much."

"So why do you think somebody did this? Were you seeing anybody? Or was she?"

"Look," Mike said standing up, "I haven't had an affair. She hasn't had an affair. Tane's the most honest person I know. If she wanted me out of here, she'd put my suitcases on the porch and tell me to get out. She wouldn't go behind my back with this kind of stuff."

"Okay," Gazaway said. "Okay. We don't think it's you he's after anyway. He called and it looks like he's just after money."

"He called?" Mike said, surprised by the revelation and angry that Gazaway hadn't told him earlier. "When? Did you trace it? Was Tane all right?"

"It was right after we got here," Gazaway said. "We hadn't had time to get a drop on the phone, so we couldn't trace it."

"What about Tane?" Mike asked.

"He wasn't on the line long enough," Gazaway said. "He didn't say. Now let's go back downstairs. He may call again and we'll want you to answer the phone."

Mike recognized Sheriff Dick Mecum, who introduced himself when he and Gazaway went into the kitchen. He didn't know either of the men in suits, however. "They're from the GBI," Gazaway volunteered. "The FBI will be coming soon, too."

"If y'all want some coffee, there's the pot," Mike said. "I can't make it for you right now. And there's the refrigerator. Anything in it is yours."

The men nodded.

Gazaway and Mike sat at the kitchen table. "Now he's probably going to call back," Gazaway said, "so we want to keep the line clear. We have a cellular phone if you need to call out. Southern Bell is setting up a trap on the phone so we can trace the call when it comes, and Jon McHugh has the tape recorder ready to go."

"Okay," Mike said.

"When he calls," Gazaway continued, "we want you to keep him on the line as long as possible."

"Okay."

"Listen to what he has to say and try to hear anything that might be a clue — an accent, background noise, anything — and ask to speak to your wife."

"Should I be writing this down?" Mike asked.

"No, it's not that much. Ask to speak to your wife, then tell him you need time to get the money together. Try to keep him talking. The longer he talks the more information we can get. And when he's talking, listen for anything, background noise, any clue you can hear. Just keep him talking. Maybe you'll recognize his voice. Keep him on the line as long as you can, but don't upset him. Just play it by ear and do the best you can."

"Okay," Mike said, and at that moment the phone rang.

Mike's right hand snapped at the receiver like a striking snake. He brought it to his face. He thought through his instructions. The whole day and night had been a confusion.

He would have one shot to get Tane back. One conversation with a kidnapper to get her home.

"Hello." He heard his own voice coming from the tape recorder. Everybody in the room listened.

"Mike?"

It was his brother, Ed, calling to say he had picked up Mick and Kaylan from Alecia. Mike had to get off so the kidnapper wouldn't get a busy signal.

"Okay," Mike said. "Gotta go."

He sat at the table, stared at the phone and waited for it to ring again. Five minutes later it did.

"Hello."

"Mike?

"Yeah."

"This is Sherry Gee."

"Okay. I got to get off the phone. What do you need?"

"I just wanted to see if you needed help with the kids or something."

"No," Mike said. "I appreciate that. Ed's got that covered. I've got to get off the phone."

Eighteen more people would call before the phone finally stopped ringing just after midnight. Mike answered each one anticipating the kidnapper's voice on the other end.

"Hello."

"Dr. Shannon?"

"Yeah."

"This is Linda Burnett. I had called your office earlier today and Jan said you'd call me about my eye."

"Linda, I have a little problem. Sort of a family emergency."

"Okay."

"Can't talk on the phone right now."

"Okay."

"I'm going to be out of the office, so if you need a doctor to see you, get someone else. I can't help you right now."

"Okay."

✝ ✝ ✝

Did Tane tell Mike she loved him this morning? She couldn't remember. He was in such a hurry and she was so focused on Mick and Kaylan. She wanted to hold him close, closer than she had ever held him. She gripped the sheet and squeezed it tight.

She envisioned Mike at the house standing apart from a crowd of desperate family and friends. He was looking at the floor, alone and lonely, fearing he might never see his wife again and wondering how he would explain it to the children. Tears rolled down the now well-worn paths on her face. *Mike hardly knows me anymore*, she thought. She tried to remember the last intimate conversation they had — the last conversation of any sort that didn't involve the children. *It's no wonder he works so late. When he gets home all he finds is his children and their mother. He hardly has a wife anymore.* Tane's heart raced. *I have to get out of here. I have to tell him I love him.*

✝ ✝ ✝

"Mike, Dr. Taylor is here."

Mike wasn't sure who said the words, but he knew what they meant. It was over. God was preparing him for the worst, for Tane's death, by sending the Baptist minister to the house. Mike stood from the kitchen table and John Lee Taylor put his arm around his shoulder. Mike wrapped both arms around the preacher and wept.

"She's okay," the Dr. Taylor said. "The Lord is looking after her."

But Mike didn't believe him. If God were looking after Tane, she would be at home with her children and her husband. Dr. Taylor held Mike and let him cry.

Thirteen

August 10, 1992
7:30 p.m.

Cicadas in the woods around the trailer began their chorus as the tiny bit of light Tane could see underneath her blindfold faded. One began weee-o-weee-o-weee-o-weee, then
another joined in, then another and another, each adding its
layer upon the layers of sound created by those already singing, until the song reached a crescendo, held for a few moments, and then faded as, one by one, the cicadas relaxed.
After a moment of silence, one cicada began the song again.
Each time the volume rose, the singing bugs sounded closer,
first filling the woods with their song, then filling the room
and finally, at their peak, singing inside of Tane's head, lifting
her out of the trailer and allowing her to imagine herself alone
in the forest, lost but on her own, away from the gun and the
masked man.

One time, as the song faded, a distant cicada continued
alone, although his sound didn't rise and fall like the others.
Tane listened more closely as the volume grew until the sound
became that of a small airplane or a helicopter. They're looking for me, she thought. They'll see his car and know we're in
here. She wanted to jump up and run outside to signal the
pilot. But her hope faded with the sound, and the cicadas
started up again. They can't be looking for me, she thought.
They don't even know what kind of car the man drives.

When the room darkened, the man stood and walked
toward the bed. He turned on the radio to country music,
then rock, then classical as he searched for the station he
wanted. He changed the stations again and again. "Hey, hey
mama, say the way you move ..." Static. "Pretty soon she'll

have to choose ..." Static. "Take my life and let it be conse-crated, Lord, to Thee ..."

He stopped at the religious station. The choice startled and worried Tane.

A religious kidnapper? Or a kidnapper who thought God was directing him? What sorts of rituals was the man plan-ning? Tane concentrated on the music.

"Take my hands and let them move at the impulse of Thy love. Take my feet and let them be swift and beautiful for Thee. Take my voice and let me sing, always, only for my King."

If He would only let her feet take her swiftly from this place.

☩ ☩ ☩

Ringing telephones interrupted dinner preparations all over Hall County as word spread of Tane's kidnapping. When she heard the news, Kathy Kersh immediately held the tele-phone away from her ear and listened for the sounds of her three children, Andrew, Adam and Taylor. Reassured that they were all in the house, she held the receiver close again and asked, "Someone actually took Tane while her children were in the house? So she doesn't know that they're all right?"

Her husband, Steve, overhearing half of the conversa-tion from the sofa in the living room, was standing beside Kathy in the kitchen when she hung up the phone. Kathy told him the rest.

"We've got to pray," Steve said. "Right now."

Kathy and Steve, when they were high school sweet-hearts, had prayed together with Tane and other Christseekers often in the spring of 1980. In the intervening years, before and after their marriage, the Kersh's commitment and faith had grown like the seed that fell upon good soil. Now, how-ever, Kathy's faith was overwhelmed by grief and fear.

"Remember Elisha," Steve said, remaining strong. "See with spiritual eyes."

When the Israelites were facing an overwhelming army,

Elisha's servant asked, "What shall we do?" Elisha, whom God allowed to see his Heavenly allies with their horses and chariots of fire, answered, "Those who are with us are more than whose who are with them." Then he prayed, "O Lord, open his eyes that he may see." And the servant also saw the angels.

Kathy tried hard to see.

"We have to pray for God's angels to surround Tane and protect her," Steve said.

Kathy turned off the stove and checked again to make sure the children were all right. Then she met Steve in front of the sofa. They knelt, held hands and prayed.

Steve asked that God place a hedge of protection around Tane with the blood of Jesus Christ — a barrier that could not be breached by evil. He asked God to, through his angels, plant a thought in the minds of her kidnappers, "Don't you dare touch this woman or hurt her in any way." He prayed that Tane would see with spiritual eyes, like Elisha, and know that God's angels were close, protecting her, and that she would find peace in that protection. Then Kathy prayed that the angels would convey to Tane knowledge that Kaylan and Mick were safe.

When they finished their prayer they extended the prayer chain by calling friends and family and asking for their prayers. Then Kathy turned on the radio and listened for any updates while she finished cooking dinner.

✝ ✝ ✝

By eight o'clock Mike was lying on the kitchen floor under the table. He could sit in the chair staring at the phone no longer. Still, it rang. And each time he heard a voice he didn't recognize right away, he wondered if this was the one.

"Hello."

"Mr. Shannon?"

"Yeah."

"This is James Lester. I'm calling on behalf of Brian Rochester, who is a candidate for ..."

"Sir, sir," Mike interrupted, "I've got to get off the phone right now."

"Okay. Thank you."

Mike slammed the phone and walked into the living room. He had to move around — to breathe. He needed to go outside but he couldn't get that far from the phone. The front door was wide open. What about the cat, he thought. She never went outside. She's probably gone, too. Mike stood at the threshold looking toward the streetlights and the police barricades. Beyond the barricades were two television news trucks with satellite dishes. The constant murmuring of twenty-five people behind him in his house sounded like a wake.

He cursed and crashed his hand into the front door, and the murmuring stopped.

Todd ran from the den and put his arm around Mike. "It's going to be all right," he said. "They'll get her back."

The phone rang again and Mike ran back to the kitchen. "Hello," he said.

"Mike?" It was a woman's voice, a friend checking on Tane.

Mike collapsed into a chair beside the table.

✝ ✝ ✝

Bonnell Davis read her Bible every night before she went to bed. Usually she opened it and started reading wherever the pages fell. She would read a chapter or a few pages before saying her prayers and going to sleep. That is, unless she opened to Esther. If she started reading Esther, she wouldn't stop until she finished the story about how the beautiful young Jewish girl became queen of a foreign land and saved her people from slaughter. Bonnell loved Esther and thought they could have been friends if they had lived in the same time. After reading about her ancient heroine, Bonnell would lie in bed listening to Sam's steady breathing and think about how God used ordinary people like Esther to carry out His plans.

The sun hadn't set on Monday when Bonnell dressed for bed and went to her Bible. All afternoon she had tried to work herself out of her distressed state, walking all the way to the highway and back, then looking for anything she could pick from the late summer garden. Bonnell had fought these bouts of depression since her father's death, but none had rendered her so helpless. Sam, who had grown accustomed to occasional quiet dinners over the previous three weeks, thought his wife was unusually self-absorbed and asked if he could do anything.

"No," Bonnell said, "maybe if I just read some and go on to sleep I'll feel better tomorrow."

She read several pages from her Bible, then turned out the light and tried to pray. Unable to control her wandering thoughts and focus on her prayer, she tried to relax and fall asleep. Two hours later she lay silent, listening as Sam tiptoed into the dark bedroom and put on his pajamas. He sat as softly as possible on the other side of the bed, then put his legs under the sheets and touched Bonnell gently on the shoulder. She didn't speak. Instead she continued to listen until Sam's rhythmic breathing told her he was sleeping. She rolled over and tried to get comfortable — to find a position that would allow her to sleep. She moved carefully so she wouldn't disturb Sam. She adjusted her pillow, rolled onto her side and pulled her knees up. A few minutes later she straightened her legs and rolled onto her back. She thought about getting up and going to the living room, but decided that sleep surely would come soon. She looked at the clock. 12:43.

✝ ✝ ✝

Judy Mecum leaned against the doorway to the Shannon's den, her eyes fixed on the rocking horse. What would happen to the children? They need their mother. She prayed again for Tane's safety — for God's protection. She had been in almost constant prayer since she arrived at the Shannon home several hours earlier. John Attaway's voice snapped her out.

"Tane's mother was hoping you might have a minute to talk with her," he said.

She nodded and thought, focus. Stay focused.

A career law enforcement officer who was married to

the sheriff, Captain Judy Mecum had the soft edges and quiet voice of a first-grade teacher. The mother of four would have looked as comfortable wearing ruffles as she did carrying a badge. One of four captains on the force, she had made a career of protecting children, creating the juvenile investigations unit before being tapped to direct the entire criminal investigations division. In more than twenty years with the department she had seen children molested, abused, neglected and murdered. Every time, she wanted to scream, "No! Not another one!" At the police academy, however, she had learned to separate her emotions from her profession, at least outwardly. Otherwise she might panic and lose her ability to think rationally.

Like her husband, Captain Mecum believed that daily, continual prayer helped her meet her professional responsibilities. Often before interviewing a child who had been victimized, she asked the Lord to direct her with the proper questions or to strengthen her in the face of tragedy.

She offered a quick prayer for Tane's mother before she walked into the living room where Brenda sat on the floor holding a picture of Kaylan and Mick.

"Judy, is she going to be all right?" Brenda asked.

Captain Mecum knelt and made a conscious effort to look her in the eye. "She's out there and she's fine," she said, reaching to take Brenda's trembling hand. Brenda's red, swollen eyes looked directly into hers, searching for assurance.

"Tane's a strong girl," she added. "Plus, whoever has her needs her alive to get a ransom. They can't afford to hurt her. We have the GBI and the FBI helping us do everything we can to get her back. We'll find her."

She spoke the words with a confidence that encouraged her. She believed God was with Tane and she would come home safe.

"You have to find her," Brenda said, looking at the picture of her grandchildren. "You just have to."

Judy wanted to wrap her arms around Brenda, to cry

with her for the fear of losing of her daughter. But if she cracked, who would Brenda lean on? Who would direct the investigation? She squeezed Brenda's hand and turned away.

✝ ✝ ✝

One person, without knowing it, held the key to identifying Tane's kidnapper. But the information was more than ten years old and the man who held it didn't even know yet that Tane was gone. He had been on the road all day and went to bed without watching the late news.

All day and night investigators had interviewed Tane's family, neighbors and close friends, searching for any clue to the kidnapper's identity. They hadn't yet questioned Milton's employees. If they had, Ricky Crawford might have remembered his conversations with Donnie Radford ten years earlier, conversations in which Radford revealed a lurid fixation for Tane, then a teenager — an obsession that began when Tane was only fifteen, when he ran a restaurant just a few steps from the Dunaway Drug store where she worked.

Three summers later Tane worked at her father's company, Milton's Institutional Foods, answering phones and filing. It was her first "dress-up" job after two summers of pumping gas at Holiday Marina, and she worked comfortably in the professional atmosphere.

By that time Radford had purchased Jack's Hamburgers, converted it to Don's Meal Ticket, and become a customer of Milton's. Crawford, whom Milton promoted from truck driver to salesman, called on Radford every Monday and Thursday, taking orders and making deliveries. Many days he stayed for lunch, eating with Radford and his wife. Crawford found conversation easy at first. He and Radford had grown up in Dahlonega, and Crawford still lived there. They talked about people they knew, places they went. Then Radford guided the conversation toward Milton Robson, asking probing questions about his company, his success and, more specifically, his money. Radford said he too would be rich someday.

The Meal Ticket struggled, and Radford decided to change it to a cafeteria. Crawford told him, "We have a used cafeteria line we could sell you if you want to take a look at it. Might save you some money."

Radford agreed and met Crawford a few days later at Milton's. "I think this will be just the thing for you," Radford said as the two men walked through the office to the warehouse. He didn't realize Radford had practically stopped dead to stare at Tane, who was talking on the telephone.

He opened the door, saw Radford several steps behind and looking the other way, and said, "Um, the warehouse is right through here." Radford turned abruptly and followed Crawford through to see the cafeteria line, which he bought. The next time Crawford was in the Meal Ticket, Radford took him to a table out of earshot of his wife and asked him about "the girl."

"Which one?" Crawford said, although he was sure Radford was talking about Tane.

Radford described her as the little one with the dark brown hair and the incredible body.

Crawford didn't know how to respond to that kind of talk about his boss' daughter. Radford's business, any customer's business, was important to the company, but Radford's whispering tone, his downward glance, told him this was a conversation to avoid. "You mean Tane?" he said. "That's Milton's daughter."

He hoped that mentioning the girl's father would encourage Radford to drop the subject. Instead, he seemed even more intrigued.

Milton Robson's daughter, Radford repeated. A sweetheart with money. He spoke more graphically of her anatomical correctness, then told Crawford what he would like to do with her.

Crawford's fists tightened, and his face got hot and flush. If Radford hadn't been a customer, he might have slugged him. Tane was a teenager, just a kid. Crawford had watched her grow up. She was like a little sister. Radford was nearly thirty years old. Crawford changed the subject before he lost a customer.

"So, you going to do a lot of renovation to change over to a cafeteria?" he asked.

Over the next several weeks, every time Crawford called on Radford, the restaurant owner asked if he had seen Tane that day, what she was wearing, how she looked. Each time, he made a comment about her that was a little more explicit than the last, as if he were testing Crawford, who conducted his business as quickly as possible and got out. He stopped eating with the Radfords.

Crawford tried to brush aside the comments as trash talk, but he grew increasingly uncomfortable with Radford's conversations and finally started lying. "I don't see her in the office anymore," he said. "My schedule's changed and we're there at different times."

Radford said that was too bad. She being so sweet to look at, he would have changed his schedule to see her every day.

Radford eventually stopped asking questions, but several times that summer he conveniently forgot to place an order for food with Crawford. Instead, he would call and say he would just swing by the warehouse and pick up the order.

Crawford knew what Radford was doing. He was coming to look at Tane. He never saw Radford approach her, but he was glad when summer ended and Tane went off to college.

✝ ✝ ✝

Crawford didn't tell Tane about Radford's infatuation with her. In fact, she never heard Radford's name until that fall, when the McDonald's restaurant across the street from the Meal Ticket burned. Everybody was talking about him then. The Hall County sheriff arrested him on arson charges.

The district attorney thought he had enough evidence to send Radford to prison, but the jury acquitted him.

Although he kept the restaurant open, Radford's financial situation spiraled downward for the next five years. Crawford often had to make extra visits to collect money.

All the while Radford never forgot Tane. When she and Mike married in 1986, Radford clipped the announcement from the newspaper and saved it in a desk drawer.

A year later, desperate for money, Radford conceived another plan to end his financial problems. He would need help. On November 1, 1987, he sat at a table in the restaurant with Michael Levandoski, whose mother worked for Radford in the kitchen.

Radford asked if Levandoski had ever been in trouble.

"Nothing major," he answered.

Radford said he had a plan that was dangerous but profitable. He laid out a scheme to rob the First National Bank branch down the street, explaining that he would get a gun, disguises and two-way radios. Levandoski would steal a getaway car from the Lakeshore Mall parking lot and drop it at an apartment complex behind the bank. He would rob the bank, then squeeze through a hole in the fence behind the bank, which he would cut the night before, jump into the getaway car and meet Radford in the parking lot of the Admiral Benbow Inn. For this Radford would pay Levandoski two thousand dollars and give him a new car.

The idea sounded preposterous, but just to see how far Radford would go with it, Levandoski said he was in. He made plans to contact the FBI before any robbery occurred.

At their next meeting Radford drew a sketch of the bank's interior, including which teller drawers contained big bills, and took Levandoski over there to look around. That afternoon they drove to Hodge Army/Navy store in Marietta where they bought a .38 automatic pistol, a holster, bullets and coveralls. At Radio Shack they bought two-way radios, batteries and earphones. Then they went out in the country to test the gun and the radios. Radford was serious.

The next day Levandoski talked with FBI agents in Gainesville, who laid out a plan.

In the car at Hardee's the afternoon of the planned robbery, nearly three weeks after he had engaged his partner, Radford went over last-minute instructions with Levandoski, beginning with the money.

He would send his up north to launder it, he explained, and get sixty percent of it back. Levandoski shouldn't spend any too soon or the feds could trace it.

"Now, how are you going to attach the gun when you run?" he asked.

Levandoski said the holster would be in his belt.

The gun made Radford nervous because it was registered in his name and he didn't have an alibi. He reminded Levandoski to keep the safety on when he ran from the bank so it wouldn't go off.

"Now, are you sure you can get through the hole in the fence without any trouble?" he asked.

Levandoski assured him.

The sun warmed the car so much both men rolled down their windows and let the cool November air blow through. Radford drove to the Lakeshore Mall parking lot and showed Levandoski where employees parked. Radford didn't know that the FBI had planted a car for Levandoski to "steal." He let his partner out and drove to the Admiral Benbow Inn. Levandoski drove up a few minutes later, almost too soon.

"That was quick," Radford said. "Did you have the keys in your pocket?"

Levandoski laughed but, in fact, he had. He slid over and Radford got in behind the wheel.

"Let me go to the bathroom before we do this," Levandoski said. "That Gulf Station."

Radford pulled into the station parking lot. Levandoski got out and signaled the FBI agents, who moved in and arrested Radford. Convicted of attempted armed robbery, Radford got a five-year sentence plus ten years' probation.

Two years later, from his cell at the federal prison in Atlanta, Radford wrote Judge William O'Kelley requesting a reduction of his sentence.

"Judge I'm not a harden criminal but a family man that got so far down in debt that I made a wrong decision. I should have my hand slapped, I know that, but please don't take this much of my life. So far my wife and family have been able to hold things together, but we're close to losing our home. Please help me get this behind me, go home and be the husband and father I was."

Radford was released from prison and placed on probation in 1990. Teresa Radford filed for divorce and custody of their son, who was born six months before the attempted robbery, and asked that Radford be restrained from coming near her after he had come to her home "without notice and uninvited and was very threatening."

She said she was afraid of her husband because of his "history of violent behavior" and she feared he would "destroy the house." His parents took him in at that point and he got a job as a painter and woodworker in Dahlonega earning six-fifty an hour.

Fourteen

*You will tread our sins underfoot and hurl all our iniquities
into the depths of the sea.*
— Micah 7:19

August 10, 1992
11:30 p.m.

J.R. Holloway turned off his headlights and the ignition. He rolled down the window and sat while his eyes adjusted to the dark forest. The almost full moon behind the trees scattered silver splotches on the small gravel parking lot and the lone picnic table at the edge of the clearing. J.R. liked being first to this twice-monthly meeting. He used the time to relax, to listen to the tree frogs, whose songs were loud enough to echo, and to let his mind take him back to the hunting trips of his youth or to Vietnam or to his most recent drug busts. He had a bust planned for in the morning — another crank lab. Seemed like everybody in the mountains was into crank these days, like moonshine in the old days. Anybody could make it in the basement with a little ether and some other ingredients from the drugstore. A type of speed, it was popular because it gave users a high similar to cocaine but it lasted three or four times longer.

J.R. set up the bust undercover, as usual, making the buy and gathering the information he needed for his warrant. Undercover for J.R. meant dressing like he was tonight, camouflage hunting clothes and boots. A regular mountain guy. The redneck look usually worked in Lumpkin County. When it didn't, when a bunch of kids were running the lab, he got one of the hippies they had down in Hall County to come up and do his undercover work.

J.R. had been doing some sort of reconnaissance for twenty-five years, beginning in Vietnam with the 19th Division. His job there was to go out in the jungle, find North Vietnamese soldiers, and report back without being killed.

He came home in 1970 with three bullet wounds and became deputy sheriff of Union County, Georgia, where he had grown up among the state's highest mountains, deepest woods and meanest moonshiners.

Marijuana was just catching on; not many north Georgians knew what it looked like. Riding through the country one afternoon, J.R. came across a corn field with marijuana planted between every other corn plant. He wanted to arrest the growers as they harvested the field, so he brought a plant back to the jail and stuck it in the sheriff's wife's flower garden to watch it grow. He would know when the field was ready to cut. When a hippie came by one night on his bicycle and stole the plant, J.R. arrested him, but the judge threw out the case. He said the plant was growing illegally in the first place and J.R. was lucky not to have been arrested himself.

In those days, though, mountain sheriffs and deputies spent most of their time on moonshiners and their customers. One of the meanest in north Georgia was Roy Lockaby. J.R. killed him. Shot him thirteen times. But not before Lockaby had already shot and killed Towns County Sheriff Jay Chastain.

J.R. spent every Friday and Saturday night running drunks — rednecks drinking white whiskey like they didn't have sense. Union County shared a jail with adjacent Towns County, so J.R. and Sheriff Hardy Duncan often joined forces with Chastain and his deputy, Rudy Eller. Writing up toximeter reports back at the jail one rainy Saturday night, Rudy's voice exploded over the radio. "Need help! Jay's been shot! Highway seventy-six at Macedonia Baptist!"

"On my way," J.R. responded. He couldn't let the wet highway slow him. The caution light in downtown Young Harris was black, knocked out by lightning, when he flew through the intersection doing one-thirty-five. He neared a crest about a mile farther down the road and the mist flashed, reflecting blue lights from over the hill. He slowed and killed his own lights so he could assess the situation from a distance.

Lights swirled atop two patrol cars, Rudy's and Chastain's, parked directly behind the sixty-nine Chevy that Chastain had pulled over. Rudy crouched between the patrol cars. Chastain was out of sight. J.R. parked behind the second patrol car, grabbed his AK-47, a souvenir from Vietnam, and crawled over to Rudy.

"What happened?" J.R. asked. "Where's Jay."

"There," Rudy said, pointing toward the ground on the passenger side of the Chevy. "It's Lockaby."

"Lockaby," J.R. said. "Roy Lockaby?"

"Yeah. Looks like he shot Jay in the neck. Ambulance is coming."

Roy Lockaby had vowed to kill Jay Chastain a year earlier when the sheriff had arrested him for murder. A mistrial had kept him out of prison, allowing the two to meet on the rainy highway so Lockaby could keep his promise.

The red lights of an ambulance cut through the mist as it topped the hill behind them.

"Lockaby won't come out of the car?" J.R. asked.

"Says to come get him."

"Think he'll let the ambulance get Jay?"

"We'll have to cover," Rudy said.

"Lockaby," J.R. hollered, "I've got you in my sight. You try to stop them from getting Chastain and I'll kill you."

Flashing back to his Vietnam days, J.R. kept his rifle aimed at the car where Lockaby hid while the ambulance driver loaded Chastain, who was already dead, on a stretcher. When the ambulance was out of sight J.R. yelled, "All right, Lockaby, now why don't you come on out?"

"Come get me, Ho'way," the whiskey-emboldened man said.

J.R. stepped out from behind the car with his rifle and Lockaby fired. Bam bam bam bam bam bam bam, J.R. and Rudy answered in an instant. Lockaby kept firing so J.R. opened up again. In thirty seconds it was over. The rain was falling again, making the only sound as it splashed into the mud. Rudy and J.R. went to Lockaby, still breathing, covered with blood, his pistol cocked with one full chamber left. Rudy called the ambulance back, but Lockaby was dead before it arrived.

That was twenty years earlier, and J.R. hadn't killed anyone since. Now he was a deputy in Lumpkin County, chasing dopers instead of moonshiners. He lived way out in the forest west of Dahlonega and he did most of his work after dark, often finding himself in the woods. But he rarely took time to consider how loud the forest could be at night, and he wouldn't have much time to do so tonight.

A car slowed and turned off the highway, its wheels crunching the gravel and its headlights illuminating tree trunks that stood in a circle around the parking lot. The car stopped beside J.R.'s and lights went off but the engine still ran. J.R. looked over as muffled exclamations of Atlanta Braves announcers on the radio told him something exciting was happening, but he couldn't be sure what. Two more cars followed the routine and the four drivers stepped out.

"Can you believe Justice struck out with the bases loaded?" one of the men asked.

"He could have blown it wide open," another responded.

The men gathering in the dark near an abandoned copper mine west of Dahlonega looked more like hunters than law enforcement officers, J.R. in his camouflage, his fellow drug task force members from nearby counties in blue jeans and baseball caps. They all worked undercover most of the time, trying to avoid looking like cops. Even so, many of the drug dealers in their small communities knew them. That's why they held this meeting in the woods, to cross county lines into jurisdictions where they could move unnoticed.

"What you got going on?" David Spellers, a deputy sheriff from Hall County, asked J.R.

"Oh, I got a search warrant on a crank operation in the morning. Guy's got a lab going in his basement. What's happening down there?"

Spellers went down the usual list of dealers then said, "We got one we need help on — a kidnapping. A woman named Tane Shannon was taken from her house at about three o'clock this afternoon, right out from under her kids."

"How many kids?" J.R. asked.

"Two of 'em," Spellers said. "Real young. They were sleeping at the house when he took her."

"Sure it wasn't a runaway?"

"Yeah," Spellers said. "Kidnapper left a note and he's called once. Says he wants half-a-million dollars. FBI and GBI are in on it, but nothing's happening tonight."

"Get a trace on the call?" J.R. asked.

"No, it was too soon. Didn't have the drop set up yet."

"So you don't have any idea which direction they went," the deputy from White County said.

"None," Spellers replied. "They could be anywhere. We're trying to get the word out to all our CIs to see what comes back, but right now we're drawing blanks."

The other guys went down their lists quickly and the meeting broke up early so they could get to their telephones and contact their confidential informants about the kidnapping. From his office in Dahlonega J.R. called nineteen CIs all over north Georgia, Tennessee and North Carolina — people he'd depended on for twenty years — and drove to the homes of four others who were afraid to take calls from the sheriff's office. He depended on his network of informants, people he'd kept out of jail in exchange for information.

"If you can help me on this one, there'll be something good in it for you," he promised every one.

He left the sheriff's office for home at two-thirty in the morning, certain he could do more but unable to think what it might be. A middle-of-the-night drive in his Camaro usually helped him relax, but he couldn't shake the image of two little children without their mother tonight. How would he raise his own daughter if something happened to his wife? The canopy of trees fell away from the highway a few miles west of town. The moon was so high and bright, J.R. could have turned off his headlights and driven safely. Black mountains rose on the horizon beyond the gray rolling pastures. At the crest of a small hill several monuments in a family cemetery gleamed. Some of the Davises' people, J.R. believed. Had to be. Davis Road turned off to the left right there, and Sam and Bonnell owned all of the property on that side of the highway.

✣ ✣ ✣

The trailer Sam and Bonnell rented sat half a mile off the highway, just down from the house. Tane lay on the bed in the dark, the strap of the blindfold digging into the back of her head, examining her life to that point. She focused particularly on her shortcomings and the ways she had hurt the people she loved. She wanted to apologize to each of them, her mother, her father, Mike, her friends, so many people she had let down, and she began listing her sins.

What a tragedy, she thought as she lay in the trailer in the dark. Here I am, so young, with two children and a husband who loves me and I'm about to die like this. God, this is so awful — like something I would read about in the paper. How could I have wasted so much? Oh, how I've wasted it. Her thoughts drifted into prayer.

"God, I am so sorry for coming to you like this, on my death bed praying. You hear about people who do this, who live terrible lives and when they're ninety and about to die they beg you to forgive them. It always seems so cheap. But here I am. I'm just twenty-eight, but I'm one of them, on my deathbed begging you to forgive me."

She balled up tighter and tugged at the strap around the back of her neck.

"This blindfold is sort of hurting me," she said.

"Do you want to take it off?" the man asked.

"I don't know. Yeah, I would be more comfortable without it."

"Okay. Let me put on my mask first."

Tane heard the man stirring around.

"Okay," he said. "You can take it off now."

Tane removed her blindfold but didn't open her eyes or look over her shoulder to see the room. At least she didn't have that strap digging into her ears and the back of her head. She decided to take out the elastic band holding her hair back, too. She hoped the man couldn't see her as she pulled it off. She wanted to sit up and shake her hair and run her fingers through it, but she didn't want him to see her do anything. Just pulling the elastic band out, however, made her head feel lighter.

The man stood from his chair, walked over to the end of the bed and lay on the floor. She listened hard for the deep regular breathing of sleep but heard only twisting and turning. After several minutes he stood over the bed. She pretended to sleep, breathing heavily. Acting like a possum, she wondered if he could see her. She saw him only in her mind, wearing that mask. What was he doing. The bed moved as he sat on it. He pulled his legs and feet up. The bed sank and sucked her toward the middle, toward him, so she gripped the edge of the mattress and held tight to keep from rolling backward. She squeezed her eyes shut and grimaced. Every nerve ending was on alert, ready to jerk at the lightest touch. The man lay still for some time. Finally, she heard muffled snoring.

✝ ✝ ✝

Mike was twelve when Barbara Jane Mackle was kidnapped. The Emory University student was buried in a box not much larger than a coffin for more than three days in neighboring Gwinnett County. Mike often wondered what it would be like to be buried alive in the silent darkness. Cold. Damp. Hungry. Alone.

He was fifteen when both of his parents started law school, leaving him at home alone in the evenings. Remembering the Mackle kidnapping, he double-checked all the doors every night, fearing somebody might come for him.

As he lay flat under the kitchen table, his back aching

from sitting in the chair beside the phone waiting for it to ring, the vision of a box underground slammed into his head. He opened his eyes and saw the bottom of the table. He knew it was the table and not a box, but what about Tane? Was she buried somewhere? He slid out and stood up.

✝ ✝ ✝

"Amazing Grace" played on the radio. Tane had sung the song a thousand times in church and Sunday School. Now listening to it she drifted back to revivals with her grandmother at Pleasant Hill Baptist Church, where she reached up and held Mama Dese's hand the first time she walked down the aisle to the altar. The following Christmas, Tane's mother gave her her first Bible with her name in gold right on the front. It was exactly what she wanted, a real Bible. She opened it and the pages were gray with all the words. But there were pictures scattered throughout it, color pictures as big as the whole page of Abraham and Moses and David and Jesus with the children and Jesus healing the sick. In the back there were maps like the ones in Sunday School that showed where everybody went.

The song on the radio ended and the announcer talked about it, reading some of the words. " 'Tis grace hath brought me safe thus far, and grace will lead me home," he said.

The man beside her on the bed coughed and shifted. How could he sleep wearing that sock hat?

The announcer explained how "Amazing Grace" was written in the 1760s by a former slave trader who had become a minister. "So don't you see?" he said. "It doesn't matter where you are in life, what you've done, how wretched you've been, God's grace is there for you."

Tane listened harder. The announcer was talking to her.

"He will have compassion on us," he said. "He will tread our sins underfoot and hurl all our iniquities into the depths of the sea. For He says, 'I will forgive your wickedness and remember your sins no more.' And the peace that passes all understanding will guard you."

111

What about today, she thought. Had God let Kaylan sleep so she wouldn't see the man with the gun? Had He put Daddy on the phone? He never answered that fast. Maybe that was God's compassion. Maybe those were His miracles. Maybe God would take care of her, even as bad as she had been.

Now Tane was back in the water of her baptism. In the darkness of the trailer, the warm pool surrounded her the way it had nearly twenty years early. Rev. Boswell said he baptized her in the name of the Father, Son and Holy Ghost, then he put his arm under her shoulders and slowly let her down. Just like when she was nine, her feet went light. Only this time she thought she really was floating — being lifted off the lumpy mattress, out of the trailer and away from the man lying beside her. She rose as if hands were supporting her until she was high in the night sky, but still warm, as high as the clouds, where she could look down and see Mike and Kaylan and Mick. They were at the park. It was light down there. Mike was on the slide with Mick, and Kaylan was at the bottom. They were all laughing. They were all right. And she could watch her family grow from her place in the clouds. Maybe she could protect them. She wanted to watch more, but they went away and she was back — back in the trailer. Back on the bed. She was going to die. She was sure now. But she was going to Heaven, and her family was going to be okay. God had heard her prayer and made that much clear for her. A tear ran down the side of her face where tears had run all day and night. This one was cool, not hot. She breathed a deep breath and she slept.

✝ ✝ ✝

Dese prayed for a sign. For nearly ten hours, since Todd had called her, she had prayed every way she knew how for God to show her that Tane would be all right. She wanted to call the house, to talk to Todd or Brenda and find out something, anything. But they had told her not to call. They had to leave the line open in case the kidnapper called. Todd would call her with any news, but her phone didn't ring. She was tempted to pick up the receiver to make sure she had a dial tone. Maybe Todd had tried to call and the phone was broken. But the phone was working fine. Todd had no news. Finally, she lay on the sofa, her head in the lap of her only other granddaughter, Sherri, and her feet in the lap of her sister, Pat.

She had to depend on God for her information. Only He knew where Tane was, what condition she was in. He would have to give her a sign. In the hours of silence Dese's prayers seemed to bounce off the ceiling. If God knew anything, He wasn't saying. She kept trying.

"Why don't you go on to bed, Dese," Pat said, interrupting her prayer.

"No. I couldn't sleep anyway."

Cliff, not understanding the situation, had gone to bed at his usual time. Long after midnight, Sherri stroked her grandmother's hair and looked at her face. Her eyes were closed, but still damp and red around the edges.

Sherri stared at the portraits on the wall, her father and Tane's mother, and wondered what her father would look like if he were still alive. Sherri was about Mick's age when he was murdered. Poor Mick and Kaylan.

Dese's neck tensed and Sherri tightened all over. Then Dese's hands began to shake and Sherri thought she was having a heart attack. She didn't know CPR. What should she do? Sit her up? Call an ambulance? She wanted to put her arms around her grandmother but her fear froze her. Dese brought her shaking hands to her face and opened her eyes wide. Sherri could see white all the way around. Dese's whole body trembled.

"Are you okay, Dese?" she asked.

Dese stared wild-eyed.

"Dese, are you all right?" she repeated.

"Let her go," Pat said. "She's having a vision."

"I can see it!" Dese cried. "I can see it! Tane's all right! I know it! I can see the light! There it is!"

Then she sat up and began to cry and laugh a maniacal laugh that frightened Sherri even more.

"Dese, what is it?" she said.

"She's all right!" she cried again. "I see the light. She's all right."

"Praise the Lord!" Pat said.

Confused and afraid, Sherri fought back tears. She hadn't seen any light, but Dese and Pat were both laughing and saying that Tane would be okay. Pat had her word from the Bible earlier in the day, and now Dese had a light — the light she had seen the night Dorsey died thirty-one years earlier shone again, warm and white, illuminating the ceiling first and then the entire room. When she saw it she knew exactly what it was and why God was showing it to her. Tane was all right and she was coming home. She went to the kitchen and started making breakfast for everybody.

Fifteen

"Look at the birds of the air ... Your Heavenly father feeds them. Are you not much more valuable than they?"
— Matthew 6:26

Tuesday, August 11, 1992
5:30 a.m.

Every light in the house was on when Mike opened his eyes. He lifted his head and thought it would explode. He hadn't eaten since lunch on Monday and he had slept for only an hour on the living room floor, still listening for the phone. Got to clean up, he thought. Maybe that'll help.

He walked upstairs after asking for reassurance from one of the FBI men that the phone wouldn't ring at this hour. He took the portable with him just in case. In the bedroom he shut the door behind him and stared at the unslept-in bed. Drawn to it, he sat on the corner and began talking to Tane.

"You've got to come home, baby," he said. "I'm not going to make it without you. I need you. Kaylan and Mick need you. You've got to come home."

For several minutes he sat and cried softly. Then he went into the bathroom and turned on the shower.

Something about the hot water hitting his skin, the soap and the shampoo, the gray light outside the small window, the familiarity of a day that was beginning in the shower just like any other day, helped to settle him. But the fear hung on. Was Tane still alive?

He shaved and walked down to the kitchen, resuming his spot in the chair beside the phone on the table. One of the FBI agents reminded him of his instructions for answering.

"He'll probably call this morning," he said. "Remember, ask if she's okay, ask to speak to her, tell him you're working on the money. Keep him on the line as long as possible."

For nearly an hour the phone didn't ring. The word was out not to call. When it finally did, Mike jumped for it.

"Hello."

"Mike?"

"I love you brother. This is Bobby." Bobby Holcomb was close, longtime friend. "I love you, man. I love Tane, too."

"I know. I know," Mike said, fearing the kidnapper might be calling at that moment and getting a busy signal. "Listen, I've got to get off the phone."

"Can I help you?"

"Not unless you can go get her and bring her back. We're just waiting for a phone call."

"I love you, brother."

"I love you, too."

Four minutes later it rang again. This had to be him.

"Hello."

"Mike?" It was his father. Mike squeezed the receiver hard and clinched his fist to control his rage.

"Yeah."

"How things going."

"You got to get off the phone."

"What?"

"I got to go."

"Okay. Bye."

Mike slammed the receiver down so hard he knocked the recording equipment onto the kitchen floor. A sheriff's deputy picked it up, put it back together and tested it to make sure it was still working.

✟ ✟ ✟

The room was still dark when Tane heard birds singing in the woods outside, hundreds of them, each one independent of all the others, and making such a racket that she could hardly hear the radio. Their day had begun. Her day, too, would come, the day on which she would die. She wished the birds would hush, that the sun wouldn't rise and she could stay inside the night listening to the music. Wouldn't it be easier to stop the world from turning — to stay right here, right now in this moment — than to face this day, to face death, or worse, at the hands of this man? But how could she stay here in a moment that was neither life nor death, neither home nor Heaven. No, the sun must rise and the man must carry out whatever plan he had made so that by the end of the day Tane would be in one place or the other, but not here. Evening would be grand. She tried to focus on that. But despite the comfort Tane had experienced in the night, despite her new-found belief that she would go to Heaven, she feared the journey into her last day on earth would take her to the very edge of hell.

The birds' singing grew so loud Tane wondered how the man could sleep. They were right outside the window, so close she heard the fluttering of their wings — almost like they were inside, all around her. But how could birds be inside the trailer? Surely she was dreaming. Yet, the sound was so real. And she felt a light breeze on her arm that raised chill bumps. She wanted to open her eyes — to look up to see the birds. She didn't risk waking the man.

He stirred anyway and sat up and the birds went quiet. "You'll have to put the blindfold back on," he said. "It'll be light soon."

He touched her arm with the blindfold and said, "Here, take it."

Tane reached back without turning toward the man's voice, took the mask and put it over her eyes.

"I'll be right back," he said standing.

Alone on the bed, still curled on her side, Tane inhaled deeply through her nose, held the breath, then released it slowly, silently, listening for the singing. The birds were outside again. Without moving, she flexed and relaxed her shoulders and her arms. She clinched her fists and relaxed, then tightened her stomach and hips, an effort which alerted her of her need to go to the bathroom. The man was in there now and the noise from down the hall disgusted her. She could not go where he had been. She could not bear to have him stand there and watch her again. She would rather do it lying in bed, and she almost allowed herself to let go, holding back only when she realized she would have to change clothes and he would probably watch her do that. She lay silent and flexed her thighs, then her calves, her feet and her toes. The contracting muscles squeezed her veins and the blood in them, waking her body and clearing her head without her moving.

The man returned and sat in the chair.

When she could wait no longer, she said, "I have to go to the bathroom."

"Okay, I'll take you. Just sit up."

She sat and saw from under the blindfold that the dark gray pre-dawn light had made silhouettes of the furniture. The man took her elbow and said, "Let's go."

Her bare feet hit the floor, the floor where he had lived and walked in his bare feet, and Tane wanted her shoes. She walked on her tiptoes to minimize contact with his filth.

He must have changed clothes during the night, or perhaps just now in the bathroom, because she heard blue jeans legs rubbing together as they walked down the windowless hall.

"Here," he said at the bathroom door. Her feet hit the cool linoleum. A small window made the room only slightly lighter than the hall, allowing Tane to see the floor and fixtures from underneath the blindfold. She was thankful for the privacy the dark allowed. The man didn't close the door and she could tell by the silence that he hadn't moved. She found her way to the toilet as quickly as she could, used it and got out.

"Do you want something now?" the man asked as he took her arm and led her back toward the bedroom. "Some juice?"

She didn't want the man's juice. She didn't want anything from him. But she was thirsty and she needed something.

"Maybe a little bit."

He led her to the bed. "Sit here and I'll get it," he said.

After he left the room Tane tilted her head back and looked around, thinking again of how she might escape if she had the opportunity. Outside the open back window morning was coming fast and the first yellow shafts of light pierced the mist. She could push that screen and climb out. The trailer shook with each step as the man came back down the hall. Tane put her hands in her lap and turned toward the sound.

"Here," he said. "Grape juice."

Lifting her right hand, she touched him as she took the cup and drew back quickly, spilling some of the juice on her leg. She didn't care. She hated that she had touched him. She knew every spot on her body where he had touched her, and now she had touched him.

She brought the cup to her mouth and took the tiniest sip, just enough to wet her throat. The man stood over her.

"Here," she said handing back the cup.

"That's all you want?" the man asked.

"That's enough."

"Okay," the man said skeptically as he took the cup and put it on the dresser.

Ready to deal with her fate, Tane asked, "What's going to happen to me today? Are you going to kill me or what, 'cause if you are, I'd just as soon know it now."

"I'm not going to kill you," he said. "I told you yesterday I wasn't going to hurt you."

"Yeah, just take me away from my kids and my husband to some sorry old trailer in the middle of nowhere."

Tane immediately regretted her sarcasm and balled her fists slightly, preparing to flinch at his reaction. But he didn't react at all.

"So what are you going to do with me?" she asked after a silent moment.

"Okay," the man said. "You're not going to tell anybody. Here's the plan. The banks open at eight-thirty, so I'm going to tie you up here while I go and call. Then …"

"Wait," she interrupted. "Don't leave me here. Take me

with you." She wouldn't survive tied up in the trailer alone in the woods. He would take his money and run and never tell where she was, leaving her to die slowly. It might take a week or longer.

"I can't take you," he said. "It's too risky."

"No it isn't. It'll work."

"No," he said. "I'll drive to a telephone and call and tell your husband where to go. I left some notes at three different places and I'll watch when he goes to each one to make sure the police aren't with him. If there aren't any police I'll tell him to leave the money. Then I'll come back for you and drop you off at Gwinnett Mall."

Tane sat and let the man's words sink in. What a stupid plan, she thought. This guy's not going to drive to the mall with me and half a million dollars. He's going to run or kill me or get himself killed and nobody will ever find me out here in this awful place.

"Lie down on your back," the man said. "I have to tie you up now. And cross your hands in front of you."

"You don't have to tie me up," she pleaded. "I won't run."

"Lie down," he said more firmly.

She did as he said and she heard him pull tape off a roll. Then she watched from under her blindfold as he wrapped strapping tape, the kind she would have used to seal a package, around her wrists, around and around and around. He pulled more tape off the roll as he went, then used a big pocket knife to cut the roll away.

"Now raise your arms," he said.

She lifted her arms over her head, pulling up her shirt and exposing her stomach. The ceiling fan blew cool air against her soft skin and she felt naked before the man. She wanted a towel, a sheet, anything to cover herself and her sudden vulnerability. She tightened her stomach muscles and her thighs. She would sink her knees hard into him if he touched her now. He would not have her without a fight. He tied her hands to the spools on the headboard with nylon rope, jerking it tight and shooting fire into her shoulder sockets.

She clinched her jaw and squeezed silent tears from her eyes. The man worked on and the pain continued. Tane thought she could bear it, but not if the man was going to keep her tied up for hours. She was being stretched on a rack.

"That really hurts," she said. "Can't you tie my arms in front of me? I mean, my hands are tied together anyway."

The man stopped and considered her proposal. "Okay," he said, loosening the rope. "Put them in front of you."

She laid her hands on her stomach, pulling her shirt down to cover it and relieving the pain in her shoulders. He encircled Tane and the bed in rope by tossing the rope across the bed, walking around to the other side and throwing the rope back under the bed to his beginning point. He repeated the process many times until Tane and the bed were wrapped together mummy-style from her shoulders to her feet.

"Cross your feet," he said. He wrapped tape around and around her ankles. Then he tied rope over the tape and wrapped the rope around the spools of the foot board.

"Don't think about yelling," the man said. "I've got somebody watching the trailer, so it won't do you any good. Just in case, I have to put tape over your mouth."

"Please don't," Tane said, pleading with the man she couldn't see. "I'll freak. I have asthma sometimes, and if you tape my mouth shut I'll die. I promise I won't yell."

"But I have to," he said.

"Oh, please," Tane begged, almost in tears again, "at least cut a slit in it so I can breathe."

The man didn't answer. He was standing over her, looking at her tied to the bed. Her body shook inside. He pulled a piece of tape off the roll and cut it. She listened hard, trying to hear him cut a slit. He put the tape over her mouth and she pulled her lips apart to breathe. Air filled her lungs slowly and she closed her eyes.

"Do you want me to leave the radio station here?" the man asked.

Tane made an "uh huh" sound from underneath the tape.

The man took that to mean yes. Without another word he walked down the hall and out the door. The car door slammed and the engine started. As he drove away she tugged at her arms, then her feet. All tight. The man would have to come back for her. His stupid plan would have to work and he would have to come back to untie her.

✝ ✝ ✝

Becky Bowman met two deputy sheriffs at the bank just before seven o'clock. The vaults would be accessible in a few minutes and they had to pick up half the ransom money from the Browns Bridge Road branch and bring it into town. The bank did not own an armored car and Becky thought that to hire one now would draw too much attention. The deputies got into Becky's Honda and she drove to the branch. She needed their help for security as well as for heavy lifting. The entire ransom in twenty-dollar bills would fill two large bags and weigh more than sixty pounds.

During the night the FBI had complicated the kidnapper's demand by requesting that the bank record the serial numbers. A dozen people could spend all day writing serial numbers from twenty-five thousand bills. Becky had to come up with a faster way. She called Steve Brinson, who ran the bank's operations department. Could the machine that copied checks to microfiche also copy currency. Yes, it could. Becky asked him to have two people available Tuesday morning.

At the Browns Bridge branch Becky signed a receipt for two hundred forty thousand dollars, which one of the deputies carried in a heavy plastic trash bag to the car. With both hands on the wheel, Becky drove to the operations center where they took the sack inside to Steve Brinson. Then she and the deputies went back to the main office where they loaded another plastic sack with thirteen stacks of twenty-dollar bills.

✝ ✝ ✝

"I'm going over to take Carl into town," Sam Davis told Bonnell. "We're going to stop and vote while we're out."

An old mountain man who could neither speak nor hear, Carl McDonough needed help getting to town and back. Once a week Sam drove him into Dahlonega to the grocery store. Tuesday was election day and the Davises' son-in-law, Mike, was on the ballot for probate judge. Sam and Carl would cast their votes at the elementary school on their way into town.

Bonnell wrapped herself up in the quiet morning as soon as Sam drove away. Ryan and Brent, their grandsons, slept in the extra bedroom but wouldn't awaken for at least a couple of hours. The boys — Ryan was eleven, Brent seven — spent most of their summer mornings with their grandparents. Their mother dropped them off before seven o'clock on her way to work at North Georgia College in Dahlonega. After breakfast they would go out with their BB guns or play in the barn or help Bonnell with yard work. For now, though, they slept.

Bonnell cleaned the dishes from her and Sam's breakfast, still wondering about Monday night's unexplained disturbing feelings. That chore completed, she looked around the angel-filled living room, bright with sunlight barely restrained by the lace curtains across the front of the house, and felt herself drawn to the sofa. Detouring first to the front door, she opened it to let even more early morning sunshine through the glass storm door. Then she sat down and picked up her Bible, something she almost never did in the morning. She didn't hear Radford's car go past the house toward the trailer.

✝ ✝ ✝

Tane pulled hard at her feet and tried to worm her hands loose. She worked just enough play in the ropes to move her arms an inch or two. I can do this, she thought. It might take awhile, but I can work free.

That's when the car door slammed. He was back already. She couldn't see her hands or feet or tell if they looked looser. She hoped the man wouldn't see a difference. She closed her eyes and listened as he slammed the front door and walked down the hall into the room. He stood over the bed. Then he pulled tape off the roll. He wound it around her ankles several times, then added more to her wrists. Without speaking, he left again and drove away.

She wondered only briefly why he had come back. He was gone again and she had to get out. She wouldn't survive tied up here and nobody was going to find her, wherever here was. If she couldn't escape, and she didn't truly believe she would, she was prepared to die trying. She was not desperate — not even fearful. Rather, she was buoyed, like she had taken several deep breaths in preparation for a race. She was competing against the man and, one way or the other, dead or alive, this would be the end.

He had said he was going toward Gainesville to call and get the money. Tane hoped that gave her at least an hour, maybe longer. Where should she start? She had heard about people who have superhuman strength in a crisis — a man who lifted a car off a child. Could she do something like that?

She pulled hard against the foot of the bed until the tape and rope cut into her ankles. Nothing snapped or even stretched. Likewise, the bonds on her wrists and hands only hurt worse when she pulled at them. Maybe she could get the tape off of her mouth. At least that would be something. She pushed her tongue between the tape and her lip, ignoring the foul adhesive taste. The slit allowed just enough play for her to work on the corners, first the right, then the left. Her saliva eventually loosened the glue across her bottom lip, and with a little more work the tape hung by a single sticky spot on the right side of her face. She inhaled quickly and deeply through her mouth and caught a reflexive scream just as it reached her throat. The man had said somebody was watching the trailer. She released the air from her lungs quietly, her resolve strengthened by the first agonizingly small step toward freedom. That is, until she was struck by her situation.

If the man came back now, she couldn't reattach the tape. Her hands were tied. She could move only her head and neck. Maybe she could flip the tape back across her mouth with a jerk of her head. She tried it once and it lay lightly across her lips. She was dead. The man would probably laugh at her silly attempt to hide her defiance before killing her. What else would he do to her? Violent death, which up to now had been a possible conclusion to her ordeal, became a matter of time. The images flashed. Rope ... tape ... gun ... man ... death ...

Heaven.

The word was on her lips.

Heaven. She was going to Heaven. That was God's promise in the night.

But wait a minute. What about the children? What about Mike? They needed her now. Here. Not there. God had to get her out somehow — out of the trailer alive. Not in Heaven. Not yet.

Her mind was keen. Her muscles, though immobile, would be strong if given the opportunity. But unless she could lift her shoulders off the bed, her mouth would remain useless. She pushed hard from side to side underneath the smooth nylon ropes, concentrating on loosening her arms. Back and forth and up and down she pushed and pulled, the friction spreading a fire across the surface of her bare shoulders, until the ropes loosened and began to gather just above her elbows. She kept working until she could lift her hands off her stomach to her mouth. Her fingers had lost much of their feeling and a thousand hot needles jabbed her hands when she used them to pull off the blindfold and the tape that hung from her face. She stared at her wrists, a tight wad of tape and rope that she would have to remove somehow.

✝ ✝ ✝

Radford drove his Trans Am toward Gainesville, planning to call Mike to make arrangements for the money as soon as he crossed the Hall County line. He wanted everything to come together quickly. Tane's life depended on delays.

He'd been gone from the trailer for about twenty minutes when he spotted a phone booth in front of a gas station in Murrayville, a small crossroads community. He pulled in quickly, got out and walked toward the phone.

Then he spotted a van parked a few feet away and feared it might be an unmarked police vehicle. Spooked, he turned and walked slowly back to his car, giving Tane a few more minutes.

✝ ✝ ✝

Unable to find an end to the tape, something she could pull with her teeth and unwind, Tane bit down on a chunk and pulled hard. Her efforts seemed only to tighten her bonds and cut deeper into her wrists. Frustrated, she looked again at the mass and took a different approach, biting a single strand of tape and pulling hard with her arms. The tape ripped and Tane's heart leapt. This could work. She found another strand and pulled until her teeth hurt. Finally it gave, pulling away from her wrist. She yanked the loose tape, unwinding it until it became locked in overlapping pieces, then left it hanging. She looked for another. Strand by strand she continued to pull and tear the tape from her wrists. She relaxed, then counted, one, two, three, then jerked her wrists apart violently. The tape broke and her hands slammed against opposite sides of the bed. She waved her free arms back and forth and shook life into her fingers.

Surprised at how quickly she had completed the hardest part of her escape, she now felt confident she would get away. She had her hands now. All she had to do was unwind the tape on her ankles and she would be out. She allowed herself to listen to part of a song on the radio and to say a three-word prayer, "Thank you, God," before focusing on her task. He was with her.

✝ ✝ ✝

Radford drove all the way into Gainesville, checking every gas station and convenience store on the outskirts of town for just the right phone. The van had reminded him the police could be anywhere, watching any phone. He slowed at the gas station across from Gold's Gym, where Tane taught aerobics, and looked all around for suspicious cars. Satisfied the coast was clear, he drove into the parking lot. But his nerves were still raw from the sight of the van and he decided not to stop the car.

✝ ✝ ✝

Tane loosened the rope from her neck and shoulders and sat up, her bound ankles crossed in a modified Indian fashion. An entire roll of tape seemed to bulge around her feet. Looking for single strands, she would pull them away as she had with her wrists. Her fingernails slipped under a piece of tape and she lifted, but it remained tight. She tried again with another, but failed. On the third attempt she worked two fingers under a piece of tape and pulled up. Nothing. Another approach, pushing as hard as she could and working her fingers under the entire mass of tape to stretch it and pull it over her heel like a tight sock, failed. Her hands and fingers were useless compared to the strength and efficiency of her teeth. So she bent all the way over to bite the tape then arched her back and pulled up hard, but the tape slipped out and she collapsed on her back in frustration, fear and defeat.

✝ ✝ ✝

Radford drove through town, taking a route similar to the one he had taken with Tane a day earlier, down Green Street, around to the south side of downtown. Again, he cruised through a shopping center parking lot expecting to use the pay phone there. Looking around, he saw nothing suspicious, but something inside of him told him to keep moving. Keep looking.

Every delay was giving Tane a few vital minutes.

Finally, after driving for almost an hour, he saw the right telephone. Two miles from the sign at Exit 6, where had left instructions for Mike, Radford parked beside a phone booth across the parking lot from the Peachtree Package Store. The phone was a foot behind the curb, almost in the right lane of Industrial Boulevard, which wore heavy abuse from tractor-trailer rigs. The summer sun had dried the previous week's rain from the potholes, so callers could use the phone without fear of being soaked from the knees down by splashing cars. Traffic moved slowly across the cracked asphalt at the three-way intersection on the south side of Gainesville. But none of the drivers made particular note of the man putting a quarter in the slot. His success depended on that anonymity. The realization of his plans would begin here.

Sixteen

[An angel] struck Peter on the side and woke him up.
"Quick, get up!" he said, and the chains fell off Peter's wrists.
—Acts 12:7

Tuesday, August 11, 1992
9:30 a.m.

Her feet attached firmly to the bed, Tane lay on her back listening to the radio and waiting to hear the man's tires on the gravel. In the quiet calm she tried to pray, to listen to the music and re-enter the dark room where she had met God in the hours before dawn. If she could feel Him again as she had before, she could face her death without fear. But the peace she had found eluded her now. The man was gone, maybe even dead. She didn't hear God speaking to her. She waited.

A commercial came on the radio. It was just another day for them. Just another day for everybody. They all had something to do — go to work, talk on the radio, play. She was stuck here, forced to wait for the man to come back, or not.

Why couldn't this be just another Tuesday at home with Kaylan and Mick watching television or playing outside? As that picture became clear, she saw in her mind the man at the door of her home, in her bedroom, standing at the open bathroom door, and her fear became rage against the pale, soft worm who would use a gun to take her away from her children and her husband.

Her body quivered inside and out with fear and energy. She closed her eyes and breathed deeply in a vain attempt to calm herself. She sat up and looked at her ankles, then pulled hard, desperately, with her right leg and pushed with her left. Eyes closed and teeth clinched, she grabbed the mass of tape and rope and pushed against the foot of the bed with both legs to break the spools. The bed withstood her, so she kicked and jerked and pulled and kicked again wildly, ignoring the tape and rope cutting into her feet and ankles, until her right knee almost hit her chin. The strange sensation made her stop and look. Her foot was free. But how? She stared at the tape for a moment to figure out what had happened. No time for that. With her right foot out, the tape loosened so that her left foot came out easily.

Swinging her legs over the side of the bed, she saw her socks and the toes of her white canvas shoes sticking out from underneath. She reached down for the shoes and slipped them over her bare feet, then ran as fast as she could down the hall to the front door.

✝ ✝ ✝

The phone hadn't rung for half an hour. The police had said the kidnapper would call early, and it was after ten o'clock. Would he ever call back? Had he called already and gotten a busy signal? Three times before nine o'clock Mike had answered and heard a hang-up. Had the kidnapper panicked and run?

Mike snapped at the phone when it rang. He glanced up at an FBI agent, whose eyes insisted, be calm.

"Hello."

"You got the money?"

This is it, Mike thought. Here we go. The caller's quiet voice surprised him. He expected something meaner, more gruff. He almost asked the man to speak up so he could hear him over the traffic. He stood up. "We're working on the money," he said. "I need some time to get it together. But you can have the money. We can get it."

"When you get it ..."

"We're working on it," Mike interrupted. He was pacing now — tiny little steps back and forth, limited by the length of the phone cord — and breathing heavily. He was one-on-one with his wife's kidnapper, the man whose throat he would rip out if he could reach into the receiver. Two members of the SWAT team stepped quietly into the kitchen and Mike was afraid the man would hear them. He was surprised at how calm his own voice sounded. "We called yesterday. You can have anything you want. Please, sir, is she okay?"

"She's fine," the caller said.

"Can I talk to her? Please ... please?"

"I'm at a phone booth. I don't have her with me."

"Please, please assure me she is okay. You can have the money. I will give you the money."

"I assure you. There is no problem." He spoke slowly. Calmly. He was under control.

"We will ... I will do anything," Mike said.

"I'm sorry for having to do this, but I will not hurt the girl."

Mike interrupted again. "I will do anything. I am Mike. I am her husband. I will do anything in the world. I will give you the money."

"I need your assurance that the police is not involved."

The kitchen was filled now with a dozen or more GBI and FBI agents and sheriff's deputies. Mike knew the TV stations had shown his house and pictures of Tane. They may have even interviewed the police. He evaded the question. "I'll do anything I can to give you the money," he said.

"Are they not involved?" the kidnapper said, pressing.

Afraid to be caught in a lie, Mike said, "Well, if you've been watching TV, they're here. I didn't call them. When I got home they were here. You know, I don't know what to tell you. But there's ..."

"I will call back," the man said quickly.

"Whoa, whoa, whoa, whoa," Mike said, "Just tell me ..." but the line was dead.

Mike cursed and slammed the receiver back on the phone. He wanted to slam the phone through the table and through the floor.

"It's okay, man, you did just right," Gazaway said. Several of the other men patted him on the back.

"No, no," Mike said. "I messed up. He said he didn't want police and I told him you were here."

"You had to tell him," another investigator said. "He probably knew already anyway. He might have been testing you."

Detective Jon McHugh, who had just hung up with Southern Bell, was on the other telephone with Dick Mecum at the command center. "Atlanta Highway and Industrial," he said. "Phone booth. Peachtree Package Store."

Two unmarked cars converged on the intersection and parked across the street from the phone booth, one in front of a Mexican restaurant, the other beside a hair and nail salon. The investigators watched and waited. They would lift fingerprints from the telephone, but they couldn't move too fast. "Go in soft," the sheriff had instructed. The man might also be watching the phone to see what kind of action his call generated. If investigators ran in and started dusting, he would know he was being traced. On the other hand, if anybody else went to use the phone they would have to race in to preserve the prints.

But Mike had already said the police were involved. If the cops were at the house, they were tracing his calls. Like Mike, the man had slammed the phone in frustration. He had to hurry back to safety, to the trailer in the woods, before the whole thing unraveled like everything else in his life. There he could regroup.

✝ ✝ ✝

A chair sat inside the front door of the trailer with a note on a sheet of yellow paper taped to it. The tape was the same kind that had held Tane. "Please don't come in today," the note read. In that momentary pause, Tane remembered the warning that someone was watching the trailer. She couldn't just run out the front door.

Considering her options, she walked more slowly back down the hall, past the bathroom door without looking in. Something bright yellow lying on the washing machine caught her eye. She tried to avoid looking at it, but her eyes betrayed her. She slowed and looked more closely to be sure. The mask lay almost flat, like the face of a man long dead, its hand-cut eye holes revealing surgical gloves inside. She drew a breath quickly to escape the grip of nausea and ran toward the bedroom, the image of the man at her garage door again clear in her mind.

At the door to the bedroom she stopped and looked from this new perspective at the bed, encircled by yards and yards of rope, the black blindfold lying on the pillow where she had tossed it, the sheet over the mirror, the radio playing on the night stand, her white socks under the bed. She was ready to get out.

She looked out the window and saw nothing but woods. The screen fell away with a light push and she stuck her head out. Only a four-foot drop and a small back yard between her and the forest. She backed out the window feet first, the aluminum frame digging into her hands as she supported herself, then dropped easily, turned and crouched with her back to the trailer.

Elation and fresh air filled her lungs and lifted her like helium. She shook her clinched fists in a gesture of victory, loose tape slapping at her forearms, then she closed her eyes and filled her head with distant sounds of two mourning doves, a bobwhite and a million crickets. The sounds of outdoors. The crickets were to her right. A field must be down there. She would have to go left to stay in the forest. She thought the highway was that direction anyway. So was the cinder-block building. How could she get by it without being seen?

Beside her a patch of sunlight dried the dew on the long grass at the edge of the trailer. Tane didn't see the grasshopper drying itself in the sun until she almost brushed it with her hand. The insect jumped straight up and flew ten feet or so to another grass blade where, perfectly still, it blended into its surroundings and became lost to her. If only she could disappear as easily. But her bright green shorts and blue top would shine like neon if anyone chased her through the woods.

She listened for sounds from the cinder-block building or from the road to the trailer — anything human. Not even a dog barked. Maybe he was lying. She began to suspect the truth, that he did this all by himself and nobody was in that building watching. She couldn't be sure. Creeping to the end of the trailer, she peeked around to see the building. It was so close, and a window with drawn curtains faced directly toward her. She stared, looking for the slightest movement. If anyone was watching, if anyone saw her streak across the yard, he would surely chase her. Maybe with a gun. But if she could just reach the woods, the sanctuary of the forest, she would run all day. The curtains didn't move.

A narrow trail cut into the woods between a hemlock and a holly tree. She tried to calculate the distance between herself and the trail's edge. Maybe fifty feet. Twenty steps. She needed only three or four seconds. Her little canvas shoes weren't made for running, but they wouldn't slow her.

She ran. She wasn't even ready — she hadn't finished planning and she hadn't taken a deep breath — but her short legs were churning across the yard and she was focusing on the trail. She didn't look back at the cinder-block building. She just ran straight into the opening, which was guarded by an invisible spider web that clung to her nose, her eyelashes and her mouth. Without slowing, she spewed and spit and ripped it away with her hands, hoping the spider wasn't in her hair or on her shirt.

The trail dissolved quickly into brambles, heavy with dew, as the tree canopy briefly thinned. Briars ripped Tane's bare legs and arms, pulled her thick hair and grabbed at her shorts and shirt, which were immediately soaked with the dew. Stalled in the thicket, she lifted heavy blackberry stalks with her thumb and forefinger and ducked under, then stepped on others to hold them down. She considered backing out and looking for a way around, but pushed on as blood rose into the streaks on her legs. An opening appeared to her right and she pushed toward it. She broke through and found herself in an ancient hardwood forest, the sloping but soft and loamy floor carpeted with brown and yellow leaves. Gigantic gray tree trunks were spaced like furniture in a living room, and banks of lacy green ferns gathered intermittently as if in conversational groups. She could run up or down the ridge that rose on her right and fell to her left, or from tree to tree to stay hidden, or in a line straight ahead. She chose the straight route toward the highway, knowing it might be several miles away but confident she would reach it before nightfall.

She ran fifty yards until she reached a clear creek surrounded by a bog that swallowed her feet up to her ankles. Every step she sank deeper into the muck until she found a rock in the creek big enough to stand on. She jumped off the rock to the other side, hit dry ground and ran wide open again, her sockless feet squishing inside her shoes, dew and sweat on her skin and clothes drying and cooling her. The damp leaves beneath her hardly moved as she passed smoothly over them. Like a workout at the gym, she focused on her body, her arms and legs pumping, her breathing deep, rhythmic and relaxed: three steps in through the nose, three steps out through the mouth. When she had put enough distance between where she was and where she had been, she stopped at a tree trunk much bigger around than herself to reassess. Crouching at its base, she put her hands on the deep gray bark and steadied herself.

She knew without seeing that the narrow road from the highway to the trailer lay to her left. She wanted to see the road, to see the gray Trans Am when it returned so she could gauge her head-start accurately. Was it worth the risk of being seen? She would keep moving toward the highway but slowly edge her way down the slope.

She had run another fifty yards when the road came clearly into her view — and she clearly into the view of anyone on it. She ducked behind another tree. How long had it been since the man left the trailer? Surely he would be coming back soon. She watched and listened. If she kept running, she wouldn't hear his car and he might see her flash of color in the woods before she could hide. But she had to keep moving.

As she stood, the sound of an engine rose from up the road. Here he comes. She made herself as thin as possible behind the tree and peered around as the sound came closer. It wasn't him. It was a white Jeep — a white mail truck. She had to intercept it. She pushed away from the tree and ran down the hill, gravity churning her legs so fast she had to concentrate to keep them under control and herself upright. She could not turn without tumbling at this speed, so she used her hands to bounce away, like a silver pinball, from the trees that arose in her path.

Even as she focused on the next tree, she imagined herself sitting beside the mailman. Would he continue his route, take her straight to the post office, or to a telephone booth, or to the closest police station. He was going too fast and he was sitting on the wrong side of his truck to see her running. He would have to slow down for her to meet him at the road. She tried to speed up but her legs would go no faster. Twenty yards to go, her hands hit a tree hard, slowing her but not knocking her down. He was past her now but she kept running. The momentum from the final steep drop carried her all the way across the road, her feet slamming against the pavement. She turned and chased the truck, its yellow lights flashing, the driver's arm hanging out the right window. Afraid to yell, she waved her arms wildly hoping the driver would see her in one of those big side mirrors. But the truck rolled on. Dejected, she slowed to a walk, clasped her hands behind her head and heard the truck shift gears as it sped around the corner. She turned around and walked slowly on watery knees, looking for a good place to scramble back into the woods while listening carefully for the man's car. Her hands were beside her now and they trembled. Without looking she could feel them shaking and she couldn't make them stop. She wanted to run again, to control her body. She would as soon as she was back in the woods. She would run until she reached the highway or a house or anybody who would help her. But she didn't know who, besides the man, would live this far out in the woods.

Her feet squeaked in her wet shoes with every step. Tiny

rocks from the creek bottom wedged between her toes and collected under her arches, and the backs of her shoes rubbed hard against her heels. She thought of the cool tar and gravel road, untouched by the sun under the heavy tree canopy, against her bare feet. She could carry her shoes and let the air cool and dry her feet after her hard run. If he came she could duck quickly into the woods. No, he would see her and chase her through the woods in her bare feet and she would never escape again. She looked for an opening back into the forest.

Checking down the road once more before returning to the woods, Tane saw a black mailbox and a gravel driveway a hundred yards away on the left side. She stopped and let her eyes follow the driveway through the trees to a small brick house on a hill — a regular house where regular people lived. Would anybody be home this time of day?

She ran twenty yards and stopped. The front door looked open except for a glass storm door. She looked as far up the road as she could see. No car coming, so she ran hard, the balls of her feet barely touching the ground. She veered into the driveway, up the hill, across the yard and up four steps to the front porch.

Tempted to pull open the door and rush inside, she stood a moment to catch her breath. A woman sat on the sofa with her back to the door. Tane knocked on the glass door and the woman turned quickly, startled. She stood and hesitated momentarily when she saw Tane, whose legs and arms and shoulders bled from the briars. Leaves were tangled in Tane's long hair, and her shorts and shirt were drenched with dew and sweat.

"Please! Please! I won't hurt you," Tane said. She didn't know if the woman would open the door or lock it.

The woman was shorter than Tane, slightly plump — a cherub's body type — with a round face and glasses. When she opened the door, Tane's words rushed out. "I've been kidnapped! I escaped and I need help! Please let me in."

"Oh, my gosh! Come in! Come in!" the woman said.

"I'm Tane Shannon," she said, breathing hard after every phrase. "I was tied up in a trailer about a mile down the road and I got out and the man said he is coming back and he has a gun and he'll probably be back soon. Please call the police. Hide me somewhere. Don't let him see me in here."

A boy who would later introduce himself as Ryan emerged from the a bedroom just ahead of his younger brother. "What's going on, Nannie?" he asked.

"This lady needs help," the boys' grandmother said. "Lock all the doors real quick."

They ran together to the kitchen door as Ryan asked over his shoulder, "What happened?"

"She was kidnapped and the man is coming back."

"You want us to get our guns?" Ryan asked after he had locked the door.

"Yes. Yes. Do that," the grandmother said.

Ryan, who was taller than Tane, slender and wore glasses, hurried to the closet where his grandfather's twelve-gauge shotgun and his own four-ten were stored. He loaded both of them with shells from the drawer, giving his little brother the smaller gun, and they went to the dining room window to crouch and wait.

"She looks like Jane from the Tarzan movie," Brent whispered to his brother when they had settled into position.

"I need to hide," Tane said. "Where can I hide?"

"Well, let's see," the woman said. "You can hide on the steps down to the basement. The door is right here in the kitchen."

Tane walked quickly to the kitchen. "This door?" she asked.

"Yes, that's the one," the woman said.

"Okay. Now please call 911 before he comes back looking for me."

"We don't have 911," the woman said as she flipped through the phone book looking for the sheriff's department number. "Let's see, six eight four seven."

Tane peeked from behind the door. She was struck by how slowly the woman spoke, even in her excitement. "Hello, this is Bonnell Davis," she said into the receiver. Then she turned toward Tane. "What did you say your name was, honey?"

✝ ✝ ✝

J.R. Holloway walked through the Lumpkin County sheriff's office to get the paperwork to serve a search warrant when he heard the dispatcher say, "Kidnapping! Where?"

"I know about it, Peggy," J.R. said. "Where is she?"

Peggy Horton spoke to the caller. "Okay, calm down. Now who did you say this is?"

J.R. stood over the dispatcher waiting for the answer.

"Oh, Mrs. Davis," Peggy said, "I didn't recognize your voice." She turned to J.R. "It's Bonnell Davis. She says a girl just escaped and ran to her house."

"Tell Mrs. Davis I'm on my way," J.R. said as he ran toward the door. "And tell Marvin to get right out there in a marked car, too. And Mason and Hawk."

J.R. pushed his black Camaro hard when he hit the highway. He had to get to the Davises' house before the kidnapper, and he didn't know how much time he had. He made the five-mile drive in a little over three minutes, concentrating on the road and thinking about Bonnell and Sam Davis. He and had known them for more than ten years. They were good people. He pictured their little brick house set on a hill up from the narrow road and determined how he would keep them out of any crossfire if the kidnapper came in shooting.

He went through the same routine before every drug bust, reviewing all he knew about the layout, playing out possible reactions by the dopers and deciding how he could protect any kids that might be around. J.R. would rather take a shot himself than get a kid shot, even if it was a doper's kid. He felt the same way about Bonnell Davis and the kidnapped girl in this case.

✝ ✝ ✝

Bonnell handed the receiver to Tane, who still hid behind the door. "The operator wants to talk to you," she said.

Before Peggy Horton could say anything, Tane said, "I'm
Tane Shannon from Gainesville. I've been kidnapped. Please
get me out of here."

Peggy asked if Tane was all right, if she needed an ambulance. When Tane assured her that she was fine, just scared
that the man was coming back, the dispatcher said, "The deputies ought to be there in just a minute or so. You'll be all right."

Tane gave the receiver back to Bonnell to hang up and,
feeling safer, pushed the door open. "Could you get some
scissors and cut this tape off?" she asked.

"I don't know," Bonnell said. "Maybe you should leave
it on until the law enforcement people get here. They might
want to see it on you. But I'll do anything else I can for you."

"Can you wash the blood off these cuts?"

"I think you'd better wait to wash up too much. I'll get
some peroxide to clean them a little."

Bonnell went to the bathroom and came back with a
brown bottle and a handful of cotton balls.

"Where did you say you were held?" she asked as she
cleaned the cuts.

Tane could feel herself relaxing slowly as the woman
worked, the way she did when she was little and her mother
fixed her scrapes. "In a trailer about a mile down the road, I
think."

Her shoes were wet and muddy and Bonnell knew about
some trailers across the river. "So did you cross the river?"
she asked.

"No," Tane said. "I ran through some marshy stuff."

"You didn't cross the river?"

"No, ma'am."

If she didn't cross the river, Bonnell thought, there's only
one trailer between here and there, ours. "What did the trailer
look like?" she asked.

"It's kind of yellow with burnt orange carpet."

Bonnell put down the peroxide and looked up. "Did it have a fan over the bed?"

"Yes, it did."

"Oh, I'm so sorry," Bonnell said. "That's our trailer. I just rented it to a man this weekend. He must be the one who took you."

"Was it the guy in the Trans Am?" Ryan asked from dining room.

"Must be," Bonnell said. "The girl said she was in a trailer on this side of the river, and that's the only one."

A black Camaro, followed closely by a sheriff's department car, came down the road and turned into the driveway.

"The law's here," Ryan hollered.

Tane breathed deeply to avoid crying again and stepped out into the kitchen.

J.R.'s Camaro took the curves well, but not the bumps as he pulled hard into the Davises' driveway and accelerated up the hill. He parked behind the house and ran to the kitchen door. Bonnell unlocked and opened the door and Tane looked up at J.R. Holloway. She wanted to hug him, this man who would protect her. Instead she cried. He was so sure of himself. He stood six-feet-four in his camouflage and boots and showed Tane his badge with his big right hand. Marvin Vanderventer, in uniform, came in right behind him.

"You're Tane Shannon?" J.R. asked.

"Yes sir."

"Where's the guy who kidnapped you?"

"I don't know. He left in his car and said he'd be coming back. That was a while ago."

"Where was he holding you?"

"In a trailer down the road," she said.

Bonnell spoke up. "I think they must have been in that trailer we rent down by Mike and Vera's house."

"Oh, yeah, I know the one," J.R. said.

Louis Mason and Steve Hawk drove to the back of the house. The four deputies conferred briefly outside. They decided to put Vanderventer in the marked car on the road near the trailer.

"Be sure to go far enough so he can't see you until after he passes the driveway," J.R. said. "I'll come down and block him after he passes."

J.R. parked his Camaro behind a giant boxwood about halfway down the driveway, then he, Hawk and Mason went back inside to continue questioning Tane and to wait.

"If he starts toward the house for whatever reason," Hawk said, "go to the closet until we tell you to leave."

From their positions by the window Ryan and Brent watched Vanderventer position the marked car. J.R. broke off his questioning to call the Hall County sheriff's office.

"We got Tane Shannon," he said when he had Dick Mecum on the line. "She's at a house up here in Lumpkin County. It's just off Highway 52 west of Dahlonega."

"Papa's coming!" Ryan hollered from the dining room. "Papa's coming down the road."

"Hang on a minute," J.R. said to Mecum. "Who's Papa?" he asked Bonnell.

"That's my husband, Sam," she said.

"Oh, no," he said. Lifting the receiver again he said, "I have to go. Here's the girl."

J.R. handed the receiver to Tane, then he and Mason ran down the driveway to intercept Sam Davis, who was returning from town in his pickup truck. When they reached him he had parked in the driveway directly in front of J.R.'s car.

"Move your truck! Move your truck!" J.R. and Mason both yelled at the man. "We have a kidnapping victim inside and the kidnapper is coming back."

"What?" Sam asked. "Bonnell's been kidnapped? Where? Why?"

"No, no, just move your truck out of the way," J.R. said.

"Sam cranked the truck and threw it into reverse, skidding off the driveway and flattening the Christmas tree he and Bonnell had planted the previous winter. J.R. realized he had excited the man and went to the window to calm him.

"It's okay, it's okay," he said. "Mrs. Davis is inside. But we need for you to move your truck around behind the house."

Sam hit the accelerator and spun in the mud before one tire caught the driveway. He jerked the truck to the left to get around J.R.'s car and didn't slow down until he was behind the house. J.R. and Hawk jogged back up to the house to make sure he was all right. Sam got out of the truck and the three men walked into the kitchen together. Bonnell was about to explain what was happening when Ryan and Brent saw the gray Trans Am roll slowly down the road from the highway.

"There he is. There he is!" Brent told his brother in a hushed but excited tone.

"Here he comes if you want to get him," Ryan called out.

Mason ran out the front door yelling to Vanderventer, "That's him! That's him!"

J.R. ran right behind him to his Camaro. He accelerated down the driveway to the road and turned hard to the right. Vanderventer was already standing at the window of the Trans Am with his pistol drawn.

Three deputies and three pistols pointed at the car and its driver, who sat pale and motionless, both hands frozen to the steering wheel.

"That's right," J.R. said. "Keep your hands on the wheel."

Vanderventer opened the car door. "Now get out real slow," he said.

When the man didn't move, Vanderventer put his hand under his arm as if to lift him out. The man put his left foot on the pavement and slid out.

"Both hands on top of the car," J.R. said.

Vanderventer searched him, finding only a bottle of nitroglycerine pills in his pocket, which he put on top of the car, then read him his rights. As J.R. called on his radio for a deputy to take the man to jail, the man clutched his chest and fell to the ground gagging.

"Give me … nitro … glycerine," he whispered.

"Give me a break," J.R. said.

Vanderventer gave the man his pills and J.R. got back on the radio. "Make that an ambulance," he said. "The guy thinks he's having a heart attack."

✝ ✝ ✝

For more than an hour after the kidnapper hung up Mike alternately paced and sat. His one chance to bring Tane home alive and he had blown it. How could he have been so stupid.

At seven minutes past eleven the phone rang and he pounced on it. He was getting another chance.

"Hello."

"Hello, Mike?" It wasn't the man. Just somebody calling for news. Not now. Especially not now.

"Yeah," Mike said.

"This is Sheriff Mecum."

"Okay."

"Good news."

A lightness lifted Mike from his chair. "What?"

"We just picked her up."

"You got her?"

"We got her."

"Thank God! Is she okay?"

"She's got a few scratches on her …" The kitchen erupted with whoops and hollers that spilled into the den and the living room as the news spread quickly. Mike could barely hear the sheriff.

"She's okay?" he asked.

"She's upset."

"But she's okay? Thank God! Thank God! Thank you so much. God almighty, thank you. Where is she?"

The sheriff explained that she was in Lumpkin County and that a deputy or the FBI would be bringing her back soon.

✝ ✝ ✝

J.R. Holloway stuck his head in the front door and said, "We got him. We're going down to secure the trailer."

"When's my family coming?" Tane asked.

"I'm not sure they know yet," Mason said.

"Oh, honey," Bonnell said, "I'm sorry. I should have told you to call your family."

"We need to call Sheriff Mecum back first," J.R. said, "so they can come get this guy."

J.R. gave the sheriff details and directions to the hospital and the Davises' house. Then he put Tane on the line. She assured him that she was all right — that she just wanted to go home. Then she dialed her own number, her finger trembling.

"Hello," Mike said.

She had thought she would never hear that voice again. Now she couldn't think of what to say.

"Mike?"

"Yeah," he said hopefully. He thought the shaking voice was hers.

"What are you doing?"

"Baby, you all right?" She heard commotion in the background

"Yeah," she said.

"Huh?"

"I am." Her voice was so weak, so quiet. Mike worried.

"Are you okay? Did he hurt you?"

Choking on her tears, she said, "I got bruised and all cut up and ran to these people's house …"

"Hush, hush," Mike said to the crowd in the kitchen.

"I ran to these people's house and they're taking care of me."

Suddenly everybody in the room was listening to Tane and Mike. McHugh reached over and turned off the recorder.

✝ ✝ ✝

Tane hung up the phone and looked around. She, too, had an audience. Bonnell and Sam Davis, Ryan and Brent, and Louis Mason all stood in the living room watching her. Conscious of her ragged appearance, she looked away. A picture on the wall caught her eye. It was a black and white drawing of an angel carrying a little girl. Tane squinted to see it more clearly. The angel was carrying the girl up into the night sky, cradling her and protecting her from things below. She was carrying the girl to Heaven. Tane remembered her vision. She had felt like that little girl, lifted up and away. She wanted to look closer, to ask the lady about the picture, but she didn't.

Bonnell said, "Come on in here, honey. Come sit on the sofa."

Tane's wet shoes squeaked on the kitchen floor and rubbed her feet uncomfortably. She glanced at the carpet by the front door to see if she had tracked in mud. All clean. She sat and looked around at more of the Bonnell's angels — another in a picture on the wall, one on a side table and one on the coffee table.

"So how did you get here?" Mason asked.

"I ran through the woods from a trailer," she said.

"I mean yesterday," he said. "How did you get up here?"

✝ ✝ ✝

If he had driven any faster from Gainesville to Dahlonega, Lieutenant John Attaway might have passed the kidnapper. He called on his radio for directions as soon as he was in range of the Lumpkin County Sheriff's Department, and turned down Davis Road five minutes behind the Trans Am. He drove up to the house first and ran to the door, where he found Tane and a Lumpkin County deputy sitting in the Davises' living room.

One look at Tane's eyes told him she was all right. They were red from crying, but a sparkle shone through the fatigue.

"Do you need a hospital or a doctor?" he asked.

"I'm fine now," she said.

With that assurance, he went back out and jogged down

the hill to the little road. Twenty yards from the Trans Am he saw Holloway and Vanderventer with the man they had arrested. The sight of Donnie Ray Radford stopped him dead in his tracks, for he had participated in Radford's two previous arrests and had long ago classified him as a "juvenile criminal mind." Kidnapping was dangerous stuff — a new league. She might have been safer with a professional criminal than with this guy, who's messed up everything he tried. He might have gotten her killed. Then again, she wouldn't have escaped from a professional. God was watching over this little girl, he thought.

Attaway walked down to the car and shook hands with Holloway and Vanderventer. He looked directly at Radford long enough to let him know he remembered exactly who he was. But he didn't speak.

✝ ✝ ✝

Tane looked like a little girl playing dress-up when she left Bonnell's house with two FBI agents. Agent Glenn Hunter had given her his suit jacket, which draped over her shoulders and hung almost to her knees. Her hands were lost somewhere in the sleeves. She would be hot wearing a coat in the middle of summer, but when Hunter had said the TV people might be waiting for her in town, she realized how little of herself her shorts and tank top covered.

Hunter opened the back door of his sedan for her. He drove and Agent Barry Witrick rode up front.

"Do you know where my house is?" Tane asked.

"Yes," Hunter said as he reached for the air conditioner, "but we have to go to the detention center first. You'll have to be interviewed there."

"Oh," she said, sinking into the corner against the door. She just wanted to go home.

The bouncing car jostled Tane as Hunter turned out of Bonnell's driveway toward the highway. In the other direction yellow crime scene tape hung across the road and blew in the light breeze. Just beyond it the gray Trans Am sat empty.

The deputies had already taken her kidnapper away. Tane looked toward the highway.

"It seemed like the road was a lot longer than this coming in," she said as the car emerged from the trees at the main road. Hunter turned right and accelerated hard, pushing her against the seat. The bright sunlight stung so Tane shut her eyes. Her sunglasses were back home in the Jeep. She opened her eyes again slowly but not completely.

"How far is it back to Gainesville?" she asked.

"Forty miles or so," Hunter said. "We're on the other side of Dahlonega. But we'll get you back soon. Got enough air back there?"

"Yeah, I'm fine."

She rolled up the jacket sleeves and thought of sleeping. She needed to get her bearings first — to see a familiar landmark. She had visited Dahlonega several times, so she should recognize something soon.

A bypass road skirted town and put them on Highway 60. Tane knew this intersection. There was McDonald's, and the Pizza Hut was just over the hill. She was going home.

✝ ✝ ✝

Donnie Ray Radford sat shirtless on an examination table at Saint Joseph's Hospital in Dahlonega awaiting the results of his electrocardiogram, his shoulders slumped and his partially shaved salt-pork white chest still smeared with clear jelly. Major Tony Carter, after talking in the hall with the doctor who performed the EKG and with Deputy John Marshall at the door, stepped in and introduced himself. The deputy followed him.

Carter seemed to overpower Radford without touching him. Only an inch taller than Radford, the major stood military straight, his shirt tight at his barrel chest and bulging shoulders.

"You feeling all right?" he asked.

"Yes, I think so," Radford said softly. "Has her family been contacted?"

Carter, realizing Radford was incriminating himself with his question, read him his rights, including the right to an attorney. "Do you understand?" he asked.

"I understand and I don't need a lawyer because I'm going to ask the questions," Radford said, his voice level rising with each word. "Now, has her family been contacted?"

"Yes," Carter said, "and they're happy."

"Good. Maybe I'll be okay," he said, his voice descending again.

"What do you mean by that?"

"My chest," he said almost inaudibly. "If everything stays calm it should be okay."

"Good," Carter said smartly. "Let's go."

Radford pulled his t-shirt over his head and sticky chest as Deputy Marshall took the handcuffs from his belt. Marshall cuffed Radford's hands in front of him and the three men walked through the quiet hospital corridor to one of three patrol cars parked at the emergency entrance.

"Ready to go?" asked one of several uniformed deputies standing beside the cars.

"Let's go," Carter said.

He opened the back door and put his hand on Radford's head, pushing him into a crouch so he wouldn't bump himself getting in. He closed the door and went around and got in on the other side of the back seat as Marshall sat behind the wheel. The three cars, with Radford riding in the middle one, rolled out of the parking lot.

Radford spoke for the first time as the car turned onto Highway 60. Looking out the window, he asked, "Has my family been contacted?"

"No, not to my knowledge," Carter said.

"Oh, yeah," he said, turning to face Carter. "That's what I asked you that at the hospital. Remember?"

Carter made a mental note but said nothing. Radford knew he had blown it by asking about Tane before the police mentioned her.

For several minutes only occasional traffic on the police radio interrupted the whine of tires on the hot two-lane highway. Radford stared out the window.

"How you feeling?" Carter asked.

"Like I'm probably going to have the big one any time now," Radford said.

"The big one?"

"Heart attack."

"Have you had a heart attack before?" Carter hadn't noticed a scar on his chest back at the hospital.

"A year ago. Left the bottom part of my heart dead."

"Are you comfortable now?"

"Yes." He still looked out the window. "What about my car?"

"It's back there on the road where you got out," Carter said. "It'll probably be impounded at the Lumpkin County jail later today."

"When can somebody pick it up?"

"I don't know. Maybe in a day or two."

"Have I been formally charged?"

"The arrest warrants haven't been issued yet as far as I know. We'll see when we get back to town."

✝ ✝ ✝

"We didn't come this way yesterday," Tane said as the car crossed the first bridge over Lake Lanier. She looked at the mirror so she could see Hunter's eyes as she talked. "We went out Browns Bridge Road."

"That's a long way out of the way," Hunter said.

"I think he was making sure I didn't know where I was," Tane said.

Construction crews were out on Thompson Bridge Road as they approached the turn to the house. "I stuck my hand out the window right here yesterday," Tane said. "My house is right down there."

"I know," Witrick said.

"You were there?" she asked.

"All night."

"All night." She sat up straight. "How was Mike? Are Mick and Kaylan okay? Can't we go down there for just a minute?"

"They're not there now," Hunter said. "They'll be at the police station to meet you."

"Everybody?"

"I'm sure somebody would have told them to be there."

She couldn't wait to wrap herself in Mike's arms — to hug him like she had never hugged him before. To say I love you and I missed you and I need you. To feel his arms around her lifting her feet almost off the floor and to hear his voice say I love you, baby. She sank deeper into the jacket, into the corner, and looked away from the mirror.

After they crossed the last bridge over the lake Tane saw a sign in front of a convenience store — one of those signs on wheels with changeable letters. "Pray for Tane Shannon," it read. She jerked around quickly and put her knees on the seat to look out the back window. Her mind must be playing tricks. She had never even shopped there. But there it was again on the other side. "Pray for Tane Shannon." She kept looking, reading it again and again until it was out of sight. "Pray for Tane Shannon." Then she looked at the line of cars behind her and the cars going the other direction. All of those people were reading her name on the sign right now, and maybe even praying for her. A warm feeling swept under her and lifted her, the same feeling as the night before lying in the bed.

She spun around and sat up straight in the seat. "Who all knows I was kidnapped?" she asked.

"Oh, boy, the whole world must know by now," Witrick said. "It's been all over the TV news and the papers."

"Really?"

"Yes ma'am," he said. "They were outside your house all night and they'll probably be at the police station. We'll drive you around back so you won't have to deal with them."

"How did they find out?" she asked.

"Police scanner, probably," Hunter said.

Sure enough, when they turned into the parking lot three television vans with satellite dishes were parked in front and a crowd spilled out the front door. One reporter pointed and ran toward the car as Hunter drove through a gate in a chain-link fence topped with coils of razor wire. Tane turned in her seat to watch three men run with a smooth, practiced gait under the weight of their television cameras. Reporters followed right behind, running and waving their arms and notebooks. Tane was glad she had the jacket. Hunter parked at the back of the building where a blonde woman wearing a light gray pantsuit stood by the door. She opened Tane's door and reached in for her. As Tane stood the woman hugged her like a mother.

"We're so glad you're here, Tane," she said. "I'm Judy Mecum. You're family is inside waiting for you."

She draped her arm over Tane's shoulder and put herself between Tane and the cameras as they walked five steps to the door. She slid an identification card into a slot, releasing a lock on the door, then turned the knob and pulled.

"Your family's right down this hall," Captain Mecum said, her arm now at Tane's elbow to guide her. "Can I get you anything?"

"Well, the FBI guy will probably want his jacket back. Am I going to have to go by the TV cameras again?"

"Probably. I'll see if we can find something else for you to wear. Here's our door." She pushed it open and Tane stood gazing. The little crowd of people with red, wet eyes stared back at her as if they couldn't believe she was real. Her father and stepmother, her mother and stepfather, her brother and sister-in-law, her preacher and Mike.

She took a step toward Mike just as her mother ran to her, wrapping her arms around her and crying hard. Then her father stepped up and hugged her. For the first time in almost fifteen years she held both of her parents close and it felt good. But she had to get to Mike right now. She dropped her arms from around her parents and they stepped back.

"Oh, honey, I'm sorry," her mother said. "Mike."

Tane ran for him, leaping at the last step and throwing her arms around his neck. "I love you, I love you, I love you," she said so softly her message might have been subliminal.

"Oh, baby, I love you, too."

They cried and held each other for what seemed like several minutes and Tane didn't care that everybody was staring. This was their wedding all over again, their most intimate, most public display of affection. They kissed and they hugged and they kissed again, her tears and Mike's running together until both of their faces were wet. Finally Mike loosened his grip and Tane backed away so she could see the whole group again.

"Where are Mick and Kaylan?" she asked.

"They're at Ed's," Mike said. "They're fine. We'll go get them on our way home."

"Do they know what happened?"

"No. They think they just spent the night out."

Then Tane worked her way around the room, hugging and crying. "I knew you would be here," she said when she reached up to hug to John Lee Taylor.

The preacher suggested that they thank God for the miracle of Tane's return, and they all held hands in a circle while he prayed. He used the word miracle at least twice more and Tane wondered why God would use a miracle on her.

"Excuse me," said Sheriff Mecum, stepping into the room just as Dr. Taylor said amen. "The media would like a statement from Tane or the family. Maybe one of you could talk with them?"

They all looked at Dr. Taylor, who said, "Yes, I'm happy to talk with them." He hugged Tane again and walked out with the sheriff.

The room was quiet for a moment and Tane looked around at the paper taped to the walls. Across the top of one were the words, "Bring Tane Shannon Home Safe and Unharmed." Another had the names of friends and neighbors, of boys she'd dated in high school or guys she'd worked out with at Gold's Gym. Scott and Miles and John John were up there, and Allen and Bobby. And there was Jason D. Williams' name.

"What's all this?" she whispered to Mike. "They've got my whole life up there."

"They were trying to think of anybody who might have taken you," he said. "They interviewed people all over town asking about you."

"Oh no," she said. "Wonder what they found out?"

Judy Mecum opened the door as Tane scanned the sheets all the way around the room for anything incriminating.

"Tane, we're going to need to talk to you for a few minutes before you leave," she said. "Here are some clothes for you to change into. Sorry. This prisoner's uniform is all we could find, but it's new. Nobody's worn it. There's a bathroom across the hall."

Tane pulled off the big jacket and traded it for the navy blue coveralls. "Would you give this to the FBI guy?" she asked.

"Sure," she said, holding the door for her.

Tane wished she could tear the sheets off the walls and throw them away. What would the police do with them?

Moments later she came out of the bathroom wearing the coveralls and her muddy white Ked's. She couldn't wait to bathe, to rid herself of any trace of her kidnapper and his trailer. Judy Mecum led her to an investigator's office. After half an hour of questions she thought the police would never let her go. She just wanted to see Kaylan and Mick but they kept asking more questions. How did he get in? What did he look like? What was he wearing? What did the gun look like? What did he say? And on and on. Didn't they already catch the guy? Why did they have to do all this now?

"Can't I go now," she asked. "I just want to go home."

"Yes," the deputy asking the questions said. "Gazaway will come by your house sometime tomorrow to get more details. You can go now."

She felt like school had let out. She opened the door and looked down the hall for Mike, who stood a few feet away talking with Tane's mother and stepfather.

"They're done," she said. "Let's go. Where's Daddy?"

"They're asking him some more questions," Mike said. "They're talking to everybody."

"Let's get out of here," she said.

Tane took Mike's arm as Judy Mecum, who stepped out of her office, led the way to a different door and out to Brenda's car.

"By the way," Captain Mecum said as Mike opened the door for Tane, "the arraignment for the man who took you will be tomorrow morning at the courthouse if you want to be there."

"We'll be there," Tane said. The reporters behind the fence jumped when they saw Tane had left from a different door.

✝ ✝ ✝

Tane stuck a toe, then her right foot, into the almost scalding water. Her skin immediately turned red up to the water line above her ankle. She stepped in with her left foot and put her hands on the sides of the tub to ease herself down slowly.

Water lapped over her as she slid lower until her shoulders sank into the heat. Finally, she was alone. No kidnapper, no police, no stares, no questions. Mike and the kids were downstairs and her mother was in the kitchen cooking supper. Several friends had stopped by with food but Tane left them so she could get clean. She leaned her head back and closed her eyes, her legs floating just below the surface of the water and her thick hair drifting in a black swirl. Sweat beaded on her forehead.

For a brief moment she closed her eyes and decided that maybe she hadn't left the house at all — that her mind had played some bizarre trick. The bite of the hot water on her scratched arms and legs quickly belied the notion. She replayed her dash through the woods, down the hill to the road.

As the sting of the heat faded, she cupped her hands and swished them like fish tails, creating little whirlpools that massaged her lightly. Her mind took her back inside Bonnell's little brick house with all those angels on the walls and tables. Bonnell could have been an angel herself, like one of those cherubs sitting on the shelf, with her sweet, round face.

Angels. Tane pushed up with her arms and opened her eyes. Water ran off her back as the idea sank in. Maybe angels were in the trailer with her last night and this morning. Could have been. Angels would be invisible. The peace she felt lying in the bed — angels could have given her that. And that sound she heard in the morning when she thought the birds were coming into the room. Maybe they loosened the ropes and tape. How else could she have gotten away so fast? How could her foot have pulled loose without help? Now she was sure. Somebody had been in there with her. Somebody loosened that tape so she could pull free. Had to be. And what about that angel picture at Bonnell's house, the one that felt so much like the vision? They must have been with her through the night too.

But why? Why in the world would angels do anything for her? The air conditioner kicked on and blew cool air across her shoulders. She lay back into the water to warm herself and thought she'd better not tell anybody about this. Not yet, anyway. She needed to think about it some more. With her foot she reached up and turned on the hot water and the absurdity of the notion came clear. Angels. Helping her. What an idea.

She remembered that people downstairs were waiting to visit with her. Sitting up again she reached for the wash cloth hanging overhead and knocked in one of Kaylan's tub toys, splashing water in her eyes. She pushed the little boat around a few times before putting it back. Then she dipped the washcloth and ran it over her red-streaked legs.

Seventeen

They will lift you up in their hands, so that you will not
strike your foot against a stone.
– Psalm 91:12

Thursday, August 13, 1992

Tane didn't know what kind of face to wear on her second full day after the kidnapping — whether to show the elation she felt or to hide it under a somber veil. A television
reporter at Radford's arraignment at the courthouse the day
before had told her, "You don't look like somebody who was
just kidnapped." She looked too "together" he had said. She
was "together." She was free. And she was euphoric.

Then other reporters implied the kidnapper had been
"nice" because he hadn't raped or killed Tane. They thought
she should look more damaged. So down came the veil.

Mike suggested she teach her morning aerobics class as
scheduled.

"It might help get you back into your routine," he said.

"But, Mike, everybody's been staring at me for two days
now. I can't stand up there and holler at them and do aerobics
like nothing happened."

The silent stares were what she hated most about what
had happened. Tane loved being the center of attention, but
only when she earned it. She hadn't done anything this time
and they still stared.

She went ahead with the class, but she tried not to smile.
And she didn't yell. In fact, the women could hardly hear her
at all. If they hadn't known the routine by heart, they'd have
been lost in the first set.

They didn't smile either. One woman even had tears
mixing with the sweat on her face. Before they started, each
woman had hugged Tane and said something like, "I'm so
glad you're okay," or, "We were so afraid for you."

The thing nobody asked, not the women, not Mike, not

Tane's mother or father, was the question she feared most: What happened? They came close, asking, "Did he hurt you?" Tane allayed their fears of the horrible, the unspeakable, by saying simply, "No, he didn't hurt me." But she couldn't tell them what had happened, that she had been rescued by angels, because they would think she had hallucinated or gone nuts. So she kept her mouth shut about that.

She came home from aerobics and put Mick down for his nap, just like she had on Monday, and came back downstairs with Kaylan. She sat in the big chair to watch TV, but the first thing she saw was the window in the door to the garage where the man had appeared. She got up and went to the kitchen and the phone rang. Her father asked how she was doing.

"We're fine," she said. "I did aerobics this morning and they all were real nice. They gave me a basket of Power Bars and fat-free brownies that we all ate after class, but we didn't say hardly anything."

"Just give it time," he said. "By the way, I got a letter at the office from some nut who didn't sign his name. Nothing we need to worry about but I thought you'd want to know." Her father read excerpts from a four-page letter that quoted from the Bible and threatened him with eternal damnation if he didn't change his evil ways.

"What evil ways?" he asked, interrupting his own reading. "I don't know why this guy's saying this stuff to me. We didn't do anything."

Tane held the portable phone, the same one she had used to call her father on Monday, and she pictured him sitting at his desk when she made that call. She was even closer to him now. Now they both were being attacked.

"What else does it say?" Tane asked.

Milton read on to the end, more about wailing and gnashing of teeth and mending his ways, then asked, "You're not going to let this bother you, are you?" He always knew Tane had his strength — her escape had proved it again — and she wouldn't be any more upset by the letter than he was. But it did bother him, even as he swore to himself that it didn't, and it bothered her, too.

"I'm okay, Daddy," she said. "I love you."

"I love you, too," he said.

Two hours later Mike came home, checkbook in hand. Tane balanced the books for his practice every month and she insisted that she not skip this time. As always, she waited until Mike and the kids were in bed before sitting at the kitchen table with a calculator and stacks of checks and deposit slips. Every light downstairs was on, as was the television, even though it distracted her. Three times she added the amount of the checks and came up with three different answers, none of them the same as the bank's. Frustrated, she laid them aside and added the deposits. This time her number matched the one on the statement. She reached for the checks again and heard a noise on the deck. She froze and listened again, but heard only the television and the air conditioner. Her father's voice reading the letter came into her mind, particularly the part about burning in hell. Radford could have a partner still out there. They might be nuts. *She* might be nuts. She went upstairs to get the pistol from the bedside table. Mike had put it there, unloaded, after she came home on Tuesday just in case. He stirred but didn't awaken as she tiptoed into the room and quietly slid the drawer open. She put her hand in and felt the gun immediately, cold and heavy. She drew it out slowly, her fingers wrapping comfortably around the handle, pushed the drawer shut and tiptoed back out and downstairs. By now she had convinced herself that nobody was outside, but there was no reason to take chances. She finished balancing the checkbook with the pistol in her lap, and heard not another sound, then went to bed.

Six hours later she knew she was dreaming. She knew it was a nightmare, but she couldn't wake herself up. She was driving an old sedan like her kidnapper's through a neighborhood of rundown shotgun houses near the Burger King. She stopped at an intersection and a big, scary looking woman ran to the window waving a knife. Tane rolled up the window and locked the door, but the woman banged on it with the knife. Tane had seen that knife. The man had one just like it on the console of his Trans Am. Why hadn't she told the police about it? The woman banged and banged, and Tane tried to move her foot from the brake to the gas. It wouldn't budge. Finally her right foot jerked and she woke up. The nightmare was over. The clock beside the bed told her it was five-thirty. She lay in the dark listening to the whisper of Mike's breath, afraid to go back to sleep. Afraid the woman would get her.

She hadn't the patience to lie there for more than fifteen minutes before she went downstairs and made coffee. She closed the bedroom door behind her and turned on every light she passed on her way to the kitchen. One more week and they would be out of this house — away from the nightmares.

She took her coffee to the sofa in the brightly lit den, her legs curled under her, watching the door the man had come through. Any other time she would have turned on the television and watched twenty-four-hour news or an early morning exercise program. But when she saw the Bible sitting on the side table, she reached for it. What was that verse Bonnell had told her about? The angel verse? It was Psalm something. She opened the book right in the middle — Psalms was always the easiest book to find — and started flipping pages and scanning. Realizing this method would take all day, she turned to the concordance and looked for all the angel verses in Psalms.

"Praise Him, all His angels." That wasn't it.

"Who makes His angels spirits." No, not that.

"For he will command his angels concerning you ..." There it was. She felt a tingle and pulled her feet up under her to warm them, then turned to the verse. "... to guard you in all your ways; they will lift you up in their hands, so that you will not strike your foot against a stone. You will tread upon the lion and the cobra; you will trample the great lion and the serpent." Tane pictured herself in the drawing Bonnell showed her. She was the child being carried by the angel up toward Heaven, away from the serpents below.

She closed the Bible and her eyes and saw the drawing more clearly. Then, without opening her eyes, she slid off the sofa, knelt and folded her hands. She didn't know what to say to God. She couldn't remember when she had actually prayed on her knees except at church. Her mind kept saying, "Why me?" but that sounded like a dumb thing to ask God. She had been so close to Him just two mornings earlier, she wanted to feel that feeling again, but it wouldn't come. Her mind wandered from the picture to the woods to her aerobics class and she lost her focus. Frustrated, she went to the kitchen and made coffee.

✝ ✝ ✝

Tracy Grindle and Kim Hollingsworth, aerobics instructors at Gold's, had begun to assert their influence on Tane in the weeks leading up to her kidnapping. She hadn't changed her behavior in any visible way, but she asked lots of questions.

Tracy and Kim were committed Christians who didn't mind if other people knew. Their example was the type Tane said she wanted to follow but never did. Now she thought about them every morning as she read her Bible.

She recalled her conversation with Tracy about T-bottoms, a thong-type leotard that, if it were not for tights, would hide almost nothing below the waist.

"Why don't you wear them, Tracy?" Tane asked Tracy during a workout one afternoon. "You'd look great."

"I don't know," Tracy said hesitating, as if she were searching for a way to say the right thing without hurting Tane's feelings. "I guess I just think, 'If Jesus walked in the gym right now, what would I want to be wearing?' I don't think I'd want Him to see me in T-bottoms."

Another time Tane asked Kim and Tracy why they didn't use some of the latest music in their aerobics classes. Both of them said the music was too sexually explicit, almost raunchy.

Tane didn't follow their example then. She had continued to wear T-bottoms and use up-to-date music. Now, however, was the time to change. She might even set an example of her own.

Eighteen

September 13-17, 1993

In some cultures torture is still practiced, even sanctioned, by authorities. The nearest approximation to legal torture in the United States occurs when the victim of a crime is further tormented publicly by a judicial system established to protect the rights of the accused.

Tane Shannon, in the year since her kidnapping, had more than moved beyond the ordeal. She had accepted the event as a part of God's plan for her life — an opportunity to face death, then to catch a glimpse of Heaven, and to respond by recommitting her life to God.

She had forgiven her kidnapper, actually pitied him when she learned of his difficult circumstances.

Then at his trial Donnie Ray Radford took the witness stand in his own defense and wove a cunning web of lies intended to grip Tane tighter than his rope and strapping tape, to wound her more deeply than he could have with the pistol he had held to her ribs. All the while courtroom decorum required that Tane sit silent in the gallery.

An assistant district attorney had learned through pretrial legal proceedings of Radford's plan to claim that Tane had schemed with him to take money from her father — that he hadn't kidnapped her at all, but that they had been partners. Worse than that, he would claim that they had been lovers. The prosecutor called Tane several days before the trial began to alert her. The story sounded so preposterous, Tane laughed. Who would believe such a thing?

"We just have to hope the jury doesn't," the assistant DA said. He wasn't laughing.

✝ ✝ ✝

Billy Watson got Monday off from his job bagging groceries at J&J Foods to report for jury duty. He figured he'd be back in on Tuesday. No way would they pick him for a jury. A fifty-year-old with barely a seventh-grade education, he considered himself shy, although he tried to make people smile. But he wasn't jury material.

Billy worked the school crossing as usual on Monday morning before driving to the courthouse. He wouldn't have missed the kids unless they made him. He laughed at himself when he told other people what he did. Every time he walked out into Atlanta Highway, armored with his orange vest, old timid Billy became self-assured. Confident. Not a bit afraid. Never had been. He threw up his hands and the cars stopped just like that. He praised God, and the children walked safely across the highway to school. No way would he have missed that unless they made him.

At another time in his life he wouldn't have found the confidence to stop traffic. Sixteen years earlier his wife had divorced him, leaving him to bring up their four children. Billy prayed and prayed for God's wisdom and strength. He loved that woman, and her rejection cut him deep. On Friday afternoons when she would come with another man to pick up the children, Billy believed he would die of loneliness. When she brought them back on Sundays, he asked God to help him bring them up right. Then on Monday mornings he drove to Sears, where he had stocked appliances all day every day for more than thirty years.

Billy was tired, so tired. For weeks he prayed for rest. Finally, God answered his prayer. His daughter was stopped at a traffic light and Billy was in the car behind her. When the light changed, his daughter's car died. Billy got out of his car and leaned against the back of hers to roll it out of the roadway. He pushed hard and something in his left knee popped and gave way. He fell to the ground and, although he felt little pain, he couldn't stand. The doctor told him he had torn a ligament, that he would have to lie quietly for six weeks and he could never move another refrigerator. Billy saw God's hand in it and he thanked Him every morning for the miracle of rest. He started working at J&J when he got back on his feet.

All day Monday Billy sat in the courtroom with the rest of the potential jurors as lawyers asked questions about their jobs, whether they knew Tane or her family, if they read the newspaper or watched television news. Five minutes worth of questions didn't seem like much early in the day, but by mid-afternoon, everybody was bored and ready to go home. The big, wood-paneled, windowless courtroom with its low ceiling became a shrinking cave. Still, the lawyers stuck to their script with each potential juror.

At around four o'clock they finally got to Billy. Knowing they wouldn't select him, he wasn't surprised that they asked him so few questions.

"Mr. Watson, do you know anything about this case?" asked Lee Darragh, the assistant district attorney.

"No, sir," he answered.

"Okay. How long have you worked for J&J?"

"Started last December."

"What did you do before then?"

"Worked for Sears."

"How long did you work for Sears?"

"Thirty-three years."

"Yes, sir. And what was your job with Sears?"

"Stockman."

"Uh-huh. Mr. Chandler might have some other questions. Thank you."

Radford's court-appointed lawyer, Lucky Chandler, asked, "How far have you gone in school?"

Billy Watson smiled broadly and said, "Seventh grade. You didn't have to ask me that."

"Didn't mean to embarrass you," Chandler said. "Are you a member of any kind or organizations like church or ..."

"Church," he interrupted, "Blackshear Baptist."

"I believe that's all I have."

After less than a minute it was over. Billy Watson smiled again, relieved that he could finally go home.

"Are y'all tired?" he asked. Everybody in the courtroom laughed. No other juror had dared speak a word other than to answer questions

"You know the answer to that," the judge responded smiling.

"Well, see you later," Billy Watson said, waving back as he walked out the door.

✝ ✝ ✝

Tane didn't understand why she was so nervous on Tuesday morning as the prosecutor and the defense attorney picked jury members. She wasn't on trial. Her life wasn't at stake.

At ten-thirty, after Lee Darragh and Lucky Chandler questioned the last of the potential jurors, they began making their selections from the several dozen men and women on hand.

"Please excuse Mr. So-and-so," Darragh would say, and that person would leave the courtroom. Or, "The state seats Mrs. X."

If the defense team agreed to keep Mrs. X, Chandler would say, "Mrs. X, please step into the jury box."

Tane watched as they filled the box one by one. One chair remained empty when Darragh said, "The state seats Mr. Watson." Billy Watson pointed to his own chest as if to say, "Me?" and Tane smiled. He seemed like a sweet, country man. "Mr. Watson, please step into the jury box," Chandler said.

Then the judge declared a lunch break until one o'clock.

Tane and her brother and mother returned to the courtroom early after lunch, waiting in the gathering murmur. Mike and Tane's father could not enter the courtroom after the trial began because they would be called as witnesses. They waited in a room down the hall. Tane's stomach growled several times. She had picked nervously at her sandwich, knowing she would be on the witness stand in the afternoon reliving her ordeal publicly, wishing Mike could be there with her.

John Lee Taylor, the Baptist minister, stepped through the wide double doors at the back of the courtroom and found a place on the second row right behind Tane. He touched her lightly on the shoulder before sitting, and she looked up and smiled, grateful he had come. Knowing that Mike would not be allowed into the courtroom, Dr. Taylor had cleared his calendar on Tuesday.

More than a shepherd, John Lee Taylor was part of the Shannon family. He had dedicated Kaylan and Mick to the Lord, he had prayed and cried with Mike the night Tane was kidnapped, and he had guided Tane through her depression that came in the wake of her euphoria.

Tane, sitting between her mother and her brother, was one of the few among the crowd not whispering to someone nearby when the bailiff stepped in and brought the courtroom to order. After some preliminary remarks, the judge had the jury brought in, nine men and three women, and the lawyers made their opening statements.

Lee Darragh described to the jurors what appeared to be an open-and-shut case. Radford had taken Tane from the house at gunpoint as her children lay sleeping. He left a note demanding $500,000, blindfolded her, drove her to a trailer in the mountains, held her overnight, tied her up, drove into town, called to arrange to pick up the money, drove back into a swarm of sheriff's deputies who had responded after Tane had managed to escape. Clearly, the man was guilty.

Then Radford's lawyer, Lucky Chandler, stood and told a different story. "She voluntarily went with Donnie Ray Radford," he said. "She later changed her mind and abandoned the plans they had formulated together. We expect to show that a scheme was hatched between these two people. The evidence will show that the only fear on Tane Shannon's part was the fear that her part in the scheme would be revealed."

Tane had called Dr. Taylor a week earlier when she learned of the defense strategy. She considered it laughable, an obvious ruse. "Don't be so quick to laugh," he advised. "He's had a year to practice his story and he's probably got it down well."

When Chandler made the charge in open court before an audience of more than a hundred, Tane remained absolutely still. Unable to stand up and scream, "Liar," she awaited impatiently her opportunity to set the matter straight from the witness stand, lest anyone believe for a moment that Radford's story might have a grain of truth to it.

A few minutes later, she had her chance.

✝ ✝ ✝

Billy Watson watched with the other jurors as Tane swore with her hand on the Bible to tell the truth. She was young, Billy thought. Strong. Pretty. Remembering what Radford's lawyer had said, that Tane and Radford had been in on it together, he looked hard at the defendant in his brown pinstripe suit. He was forty or so, wiry gray and black hair, soft looking. When Radford had stood as the jury came in he looked stiff, like he had an old man's back. Billy wondered what in the world a girl like Tane would want with a man like that. It didn't make sense.

✝ ✝ ✝

For three hours Tane answered the assistant district attorney's questions, telling everything that happened that Monday and Tuesday, beginning with her trip to Gold's Gym and ending with her escape. She described the mask and the gun and the cars and the trailer. She said she had feared for her children at home alone all afternoon and that she expected the man to kill her.

She remained strong throughout until she told about her night in the trailer and Darragh said, "Describe what you were thinking as you were lying there."

She knew she wouldn't make it through this part without crying. She still hadn't told anybody about the vision and her belief that angels had intervened except Dr. Taylor and Kim and Tracy.

"I would picture my kids," she said, and her diaphragm made a tiny, involuntary jerk. "I would picture, sounds crazy, but if you are there you would know what I'm talking about," she held the arms of the chair tightly, "but I was sitting on clouds watching my children, watching Mike raise our children."

"Why were you picturing yourself in those circumstances?"

Tane hesitated and looked down. Then she looked at Dr. Taylor, who appeared to nod slightly with encouragement. She wanted to say, "God was giving me a vision. He was telling me that I wasn't going to hell." But she couldn't. People would say she was crazy and she would blow the whole trial. So she said instead, "Because I thought I was dying. I didn't think I would see them again."

She was crying now, crying hard. Lee Darragh brought her a tissue. Later he questioned Tane about her escape. How could she get out of the ropes and tape?

Again, Tane passed on her opportunity to claim a miracle. "I was afraid if he came back and saw me, I didn't know what he would do," she said. "I didn't know if he would kill me, and at that time the only prayers I said were really not to let me get home, but just to die unpainfully. Just to die. Just to get it over with. So I just thought if he comes and he sees me halfway untied, he might just shoot me or something."

✝ ✝ ✝

"There's Mommie on TV!" Kaylan yelled. She and Mick and Tane were sitting on the floor close to the set, and Mike hurried into the room from the kitchen to watch with them. The children laughed excitedly. They didn't understand. The TV news was all over the trial on Tuesday night, focusing on Lucky Chandler's claim that Tane and Radford were co-conspirators. Mike kneeled and put a hand on Tane's shoulder, then squeezed it as her muscles tensed with anger. The camera showed a close-up of Chandler telling the jury, "She voluntarily went with Donnie Ray Radford."

"What are they doing?" Mike said, standing and pacing. "What are they doing? They act like they believe the guy."

Tane, maintaining her composure in the realization of what Kaylan and Mick were watching, stood and said, "C'mon, you two. Let's get supper." She herded them into the kitchen while Mike continued to watch and pace.

As soon as the report ended the phone rang and rang and rang. Tane's mother, father and brother all called with support. Then Kathy, a neighbor who watched Kaylan and Mick during the trial, called and told Tane to read Psalm 52. Tane wrote "Ps 52" on a little piece of paper and took it to the table beside the sofa.

The phone rang once more and Tane grabbed it on the first ring.

"Slut!" said a woman who immediately hung up.

"Hello?" Tane said. "Hello!"

"Who was that?" Mike asked as Tane hung up.

"Somebody believes him," Tane said, considering the possibility for the first time. "Some woman actually believes him."

✝ ✝ ✝

The nightmare woke up Tane — the same one where the woman with a knife bangs at her car window. Tane was awake before she opened her eyes, telling herself it was a dream, but she had to look at the clock to convince herself. The red numbers shone 5:05. Confident of her reality, she lay wondering what to do. She usually got up at five-thirty anyway; no point trying to go back to sleep. So she slid out of bed and walked into the kitchen where she flipped a switch, shielded her eyes and squinted. She scooped coffee and poured it into the paper filter, filled the carafe at the sink and poured water into the back of the coffee maker, then leaned against the kitchen island and waited.

Lucky Chandler would be asking the questions today. He would be tough. At least that's what everybody in the prosecutor's office told her. "Just stay cool," Lee Darragh had advised her. She had popped off a couple of times in his office, so he knew she had a temper. "And answer his questions as simply as possible. Don't ad lib or try to straighten him out. He'll twist your words, but you can't stop him. I'll object when it's appropriate."

She had wanted to call Chandler a liar in court on Tuesday. She poured a cup of coffee and hoped she could restrain herself today. She walked to the den sofa, turned on the light and picked up her Bible. The note she had written, "Ps 52," lay beside it. She sat and opened to Psalms and read.

"Why do you boast of evil, you mighty man? Why do you boast all day long, you who are a disgrace in the eyes of God?

"Your tongue plots destruction; it is like a sharpened razor, you who practice deceit.

"You love evil rather than good, falsehood rather than speaking the truth.

"You love every harmful word. O you deceitful tongue!

"Surely God will bring you down to everlasting ruin; He will snatch you up and tear you from your tent; he will uproot you from the land of the living."

Tane put her finger at the spot and closed the Bible for a moment. She leaned back into corner of the big sofa and closed her eyes. She didn't pray. She just thought about Donnie Ray Radford and God's plan for him — that she needn't worry about vengeance. God was in charge of that. She opened the Bible again and continued reading.

"The righteous will see and fear; they will laugh at him, saying, 'Here now is the man who did not make God his stronghold but trusted in his great wealth and grew strong by destroying others.'

"But I am like an olive tree flourishing in the house of God. I trust in God's unfailing love for ever and ever.

"I will praise you forever for what you have done; in your name I will hope for your name is good. I will praise you in the presence of your saints."

Again, she closed her Bible, and this time she did pray. "God, I do trust in your unfailing love and I do praise You. Please be with me today and let Your truth give me strength."

She also prayed for Mike, as she had done every morning since her escape — that he would see the Lord more clearly and understand what He had done for her — how He had used the kidnapping to point her in the right direction. But Mike would not understand until Tane drew up enough courage to tell him about the vision and the angels. Until then, he would see only the evil in it. She would have to figure out a way to tell him.

She opened her eyes and held her warm coffee mug with two hands, her Bible in her lap, wondering what the defense attorney would ask.

✝ ✝ ✝

Billy Watson also prayed on Wednesday morning before he reported to his school crossing and then to the courthouse. He still thanked God every day that he didn't have to move washers and dryers. Then he prayed about the trial.

"I know You put me on that jury for a reason," he said, "but I can't imagine why. I guess I'll see soon enough."

Two hours later he waited in the jury room with the other eight men and three women. They talked softly in groups of two or three. The judge had told them not to discuss the trial, so Billy talked about the food business with Steve Dunn, the new manager of Curt's Cafeteria, a big country buffet-style place just down the hill from Billy's church. Steve was young, about thirty-five, Billy figured, and had run the Collegiate restaurant downtown for a couple of years before going to Curt's. Billy liked Steve.

The bailiff called the jury into the courtroom where Lucky Chandler had his chance with Tane. He let her know from his first question that Wednesday would not be easy. And she showed him right off how she earned her reputation as a feisty woman. Even Billy, who didn't know her, could see she was fighting to hold back her temper.

"Mrs. Shannon, isn't it true you first met Donnie Radford when you were a teenager and in high school at Johnson High School?"

"No, it is not."

"Isn't it true that after you met him that you and Mr. Radford developed a romantic relationship?"

"No, it is not."

"That went on for several months while you were in high school?"

"No, it is not."

"Isn't it true that you rekindled the relationship with him in 1991?"

"No, it is not."

"Isn't it true that you knew Donnie Radford as an older man, a person who was a little more than ten years older than you and who was easy for you to manipulate and get your way with?"

"No, it is not."

"And isn't it true that how this all came about, that you were manipulating Donnie to get your own way?"

"No, it is not."

Billy looked around at other jurors to see if they were as upset by this exchange as he was. They all motionless, as if they were watching TV.

☩ ☩ ☩

Tane could not sit still. She crossed her legs, clinched her fists and set her jaw while Chandler tried to pick apart her testimony about the kidnapping. Her anger showed in her sarcasm.

Chandler asked, "You made an attempt to lock the door. What type of lock does that door have on it?"

"A lousy lock," she answered.

Several people in the courtroom smiled, but Tane did not. She had slid up to the very edge of her chair.

Chandler phrased most of his questions in the form of statements, which she tried to cut off.

"You got scared at that point because you were so deep in this ..."

"Because I was kidnapped," she interrupted.

"If you would, please, let me ask the question and then you may respond," Chandler said before attempting to make his statement again. "You got scared at this point because you were so deep in this scheme that you could not extract yourself without pointing a finger at the person you were in with, could you?"

Tane knew a simple yes or no would not suffice, so she said, "I did not know Donnie Ray Radford."

But Chandler continued along the same line. "And you had to quickly decide some way to remove yourself from this scheme, didn't you?"

Lee Darragh tried to help at this point, objecting to the question. "The question assumes a scheme, a plan, not established," he said.

But the judge allowed Chandler to continue.

"You had to do something to remove yourself from this scheme and you had to do it quickly," Chandler said.

"Funny it took all day, didn't it," Tane responded. She was mad and she didn't care who knew it. To her left she saw slight movement behind the prosecutor's table. She looked that direction and saw Judy Smith, an assistant district attorney, making pleading faces, as if to say, "Please don't pop off. Don't blow it now."

"You had to think of something, didn't you?" Chandler asked.

Tane took a breath and slid back into her chair before she answered, "All I thought of was praying and for God to give me the strength to get the heck away from this dangerous man."

Where did that come from, she thought. *I wasn't going to talk about praying. Yet, there it was, and it came out so easily.*

The defense attorney didn't miss a beat as he continued to lay out his case. He seemed intent on engaging Tane in a heated argument. She, on the other hand, was fighting with a handicap. No matter how absurd or obscene the questions, no matter the horrible insinuation, no matter the damage Chandler inflicted in open court, Tane was permitted to do nothing but answer calmly. By law neither she nor the district attorney could tell the jurors about Radford's arrest on arson charges ten years earlier, or his conviction following a botched bank robbery or that his ex-wife had filed a restraining order to keep him away because she said he was dangerous.

He could take a set of lies sharpened to a razor's edge, slice her reputation down the middle and chop it into little bits, but she could not discuss the facts of his background.

In the tension, Tane forgot her instructions to look at the jurors and found herself staring directly at Donnie Ray Radford, wearing the same brown pinstripe suit he had worn on Monday and Tuesday. He looked back at her briefly then turned away. She turned back toward Lucky Chandler.

"Was there any discussion about why you were being allowed to take a change of clothes with you?" he asked.

"I told you, he told me we would be gone for awhile."

"Did that seem in any way strange to you?"

"Seemed like I was being kidnapped."

"Did that seem at all unusual for a kidnapping to you?"

"I've never been kidnapped. I couldn't really answer that."

Chandler changed the subject and asked a moment later, "Why did you call your father when he was holding a gun on you?"

Tane looked at Radford again, who must have felt her eyes because he looked up from the table.

"It was a chance I had to take. Otherwise my kids would have been at home alone from three until eight not knowing where their mother was."

"Why didn't you call 911?"

She held her stare. This time he was staring back, refusing to look away.

"And wait thirty minutes on the phone while they got my address and name? I don't think so," she said.

Her eyes didn't move — didn't blink. She refused to break the stare. Finally, the defense attorney turned away momentarily and Radford looked away, toward the lawyer.

Chandler picked up a wad of strapping tape and walked toward Tane with it. The first time Tane had seen it, Donnie Radford was wrapping it around her hands and feet. Her lack of emotional reaction to seeing it again surprised her. "How wide is that tape Mrs. Shannon?"

"About an inch wide."

"Very narrow, isn't it."

"Narrow."

"And not the heaviest tape that is obtainable to restrict someone is it."

"Objection," said Lee Darragh, standing.

"Sustained," the judge replied.

"Because that tape was narrow and thin made your escape much easier didn't it?" Chandler said.

"No, it did not."

"Are you saying that a heavier tape would have been easier to escape from?"

Tane couldn't think of a more ridiculous question. "He did come back after thirty minutes and reinforce the job that he had already done thoroughly," she said.

"It stretched very easily, didn't it."

Tane slid to the edge of her chair, remembering how hard she worked to free herself. "No, it did not."

"It was never intended to secure you, was it."

"It did a good job," Tane said leaning even farther forward. "Would you like me to demonstrate?"

One of the jurors caught Tane's eye as she wrote something on a yellow pad. *She's writing that I have a hot temper,* Tane thought. She folded her hands in her lap and tried to calm herself again.

"You and he planned that," Chandler said, ignoring Tane's offer to tie him up.

"We did not."

Chandler asked several easy questions to ease the tension slowly, like a plane coming in for a landing, then took off again before touching ground, questioning Tane's recollection of the noises she heard in the hours before her escape.

"I heard helicopters and geese go by," she said. "I thought there might be a lake that I could go jump in and swim and hide, or a helicopter may have come and got this man and I could run. In my eyes those were signs from God that He sent to give me courage."

There. She'd said it again. God had been there with her. She spoke the words so naturally, He must have been giving them to her. She looked at the jurors and every one of them was looking back at her. Her eyes stopped with the country man — she had forgotten his name. His blue eyes were softer than other jurors', compassionate. The others weren't mean, but they weren't supportive either. She read nothing in them. Before Wednesday she had never considered the possibility that people wouldn't believe her. Now, after two hours of Lucky Chandler's relentless attack, she was relieved to find at least one person who did — whose eyes appeared to, anyway.

"You said earlier that you heard sirens," Chandler said.

"You know, it's probably my imagination, a gift from God to give me courage," she said. "In reality I did not hear a helicopter. I did not hear an ambulance."

"So you just made up something to fit into …"

"I didn't make anything up," she interrupted, and she heard her own voice coming back too loudly through the speakers.

"To fit the information, right?"

More slowly and quietly, she said, "This was a gift from God to give me courage to get away." She was driving home the point with confidence now.

"Whatever this mysterious noise was, the loud noise you heard …" Chandler said.

Tane was beyond anger now and tired of fighting. She

pushed herself against the back of her chair, took a deep breath and felt her insides settle. The truth was with her. Chandler, apparently, was ready to call a truce as well, turning toward the prosecutor's table as he said, "That's all I have at this time."

✝ ✝ ✝

"Call Dr. Mike Shannon."

Tane turned toward the door behind her as the bailiff opened it for Mike. She was nervous for him, wishing she could warn him about the cross-examination, how hard Lucky Chandler had tried to make her out to be a liar. She wanted to prepare him for that treatment.

Mike swore to tell the truth, then sat and looked at Tane. Their eyes met in a gaze they had grown accustomed to since the kidnapping — a look usually reserved for young people in love. They held it long enough for Tane's eyes to become wet. She was glad now that Mike had been out of the court-room when she testified, for she could not have looked at him and maintained her composure, especially when she recalled her anticipation of death and separation from him and their children. In the year since she had been kidnapped, Tane and Mike had avoided discussing many of the details of their ex-periences. Tane was curious but not eager to know how Mike had dealt with the possibility of her death, and she assumed he felt the same way. But to talk about it would have been to relive it, and that she could not do. Not with Mike. Not yet. Now, she was about to watch Mike relive it alone, with a court-room full of strangers, including reporters and TV cameras. She wished she could go sit beside him.

"Sir, will you state your name and occupation, please?" Lee Darragh said.

They broke the gaze simultaneously and looked toward the prosecutor, who, as he had done with Tane, guided Mike deliberately through the events surrounding the kidnapping. Mike described the phone call he received from Milton's sec-retary, his hundred-miles-an-hour drive home, and his house surrounded by crime scene tape when he arrived. "Describe that feeling the best way you can," Darragh said.

Mike looked down as he replied. Darragh had instructed him to look at the jurors as much as possible, but he couldn't look anybody in the eye right now for fear of weeping. "It's very hard to describe absolutely," he began. "If you could imagine the worst feeling in the world." Finding enough strength to look at Darragh, he said, "I guess if you ever lost a loved one or something like, then that approximates this feeling. You don't ever want to be in that situation."

He looked at Tane only when he had finished speaking, then quickly looked down again.

Darragh asked Mike to tell what happened at the house through the night. Mike recalled the supportive phone calls from friends, the police officers who stepped over and around him as he lay on the floor waiting for the kidnapper to call and tell him Tane was alive.

"I just wanted to sit by the phone and wait and just hope to God somebody would call," he said.

Then the prosecutor brought a black and silver tape recorder toward the witness stand. Mike took a deep breath and shifted in his chair. They had told him and Tane beforehand that they would play the kidnapper's call, and Tane thought they were ready. Darragh placed the recorder on the ledge in front of Mike, then leaned over and plugged it in. He pressed a button and turned up the volume. That quiet, awful voice, magnified by the recorder and by Mike's microphone, filled the courtroom.

"You got the money?"

Mike leaned forward and squeezed the bridge of his nose between his thumb and forefinger. His own voice followed, the excessive magnification accentuating the tremors.

"We're working on the money," he said. "I need time to get it together. But you can have the money."

The kidnapper's voice interrupted, "When you get it ..."

If Tane had been sitting behind the defense table instead of the prosecutor at that moment, they would have had to pull her off of Donnie Ray Radford. She would have gone for his throat with her bare hands. As it was, she held the seat of her chair with both hands and squeezed so hard her finger-tips hurt. How dare he use her, use Mike's love for her, in his twisted scheme to get money. It was one thing to pull a gun on her and shuffle her out of the house, but to use that power against Mike and the rest of her family … she felt the seat under her shift slightly with her squeezing and considered ripping it from its base and slamming it over Radford's head as his weak, evil little voice continued to blast out the cranked-up recorder.

"I will call back," he said.

"Whoa, whoa, whoa, whoa," Mike's voice cried, "Just tell me …"

The tape ended and Mike released his nose and looked up. Tane loosened her grip on the chair.

"Was that the end of the conversation?" Darragh asked.

"Yes, sir," Mike answered, almost inaudibly. "I was begging."

✝ ✝ ✝

After a ten-minute recess, Lee Darragh called Bonnell Davis, the woman who rented the trailer to Radford and who offered Tane sanctuary among her angels the morning she escaped. She told the jury that she was reading the Bible when she heard a knock at the door. "I saw this lady standing there that looked in real distress," she said. "Her hair looked real stringy and she was scratched up real bad from running through the bushes and her shoes were wet."

This was the part Tane liked to relive — stepping into Bonnell's house and seeing this grandmother with her open Bible, her angel pictures and her grandsons with their shot-guns. It was like going to her own grandmother's house, not some stranger's.

The grandsons followed Bonnell to the stand, first Brent then Ryan. They told how they had seen Radford drive back in his Trans Am as they waited at the window with their shotguns.

J.R. Holloway testified next. He was the first of several law enforcement officers to give details of Radford's arrest and the investigation that followed. On cross-examination of each, Lucky Chandler hammered away at their inability to find a gun.

"Didn't find the gun, did you?" Chandler asked Investigator Kevin Head in a typical exchange.

"No, sir."

"Didn't find any bullets?"

"No, sir."

"Nothing at all that you found would be associated with a firearm, would it."

"No, sir."

"I believe that's all I have," Chandler said, turning triumphantly toward his table.

On reflection, Tane speculated that Radford, after Mike told him that the police were involved, ditched the pistol somewhere along the way during his drive from Gainesville back to the trailer. He might even have thrown it off the bridge into Lake Lanier. But such theories are not admissible as evidence, so the officers were left at Chandler's mercy.

Darragh rested the state's case after the investigators had testified and Lucky Chandler called the lone defense witness, Donnie Ray Radford, who shuffled from his chair beside Chandler to the witness stand, standing and walking more like an old man than ever. Tane thought he was after sympathy from the jury. He hadn't been so stiff when he came to her house a year ago.

"When did you first meet Tane Shannon?" Chandler asked after Radford had sworn to tell the truth.

"Either '80 or '81. She was working in Dunaway Drugs."

The answer surprised Tane. How did he know she had worked at the drugstore? She thought hard about those weeks during Christmas and summer when she was fourteen or fifteen and working her first job, but she couldn't place Radford. Had he really seen her then?

"I had a restaurant nearby and I frequented it quite a bit," Radford continued. "She was just down there working at the cash register one day, and I went down, we started talking. She was young. She just seemed like a school girl."

This was weird. He was speaking as coolly and easily as if it were true — as if he believed it himself.

Then Radford said Tane drove a yellow Corvette at the time, and Tane knew the prosecutor could catch him in a lie. She wasn't old enough to drive then. Her mother had driven her to work every day. Still, his story had enough truth in it to sound almost believable. And how did he know she had driven a Corvette a year later?

"What kind of relationship did you develop with Tane Robson?" Chandler asked.

"We became sexually compatible at the time, I guess," Radford answered, and Tane's stomach turned like it was full of worms. You are so sick, she thought. So sick and so evil.

"How long did that relationship last?" Chandler asked.

"About a month."

"What caused it to end?"

"She was too young for me."

Tane rolled her eyes and sighed aloud, as if to tell the jury sarcastically, "Yeah, right." Radford said he didn't see Tane again until after his divorce in 1992 — failing to mention his prison time during the interim — when he came across Tane's and Mike's wedding announcement. He had cut it out of the paper when they married in 1985. Radford said he was lonely and called Tane and they decided to meet in the Sears parking lot.

"She came running over to me and we hugged and we had just a small kiss at the time," he said.

He said they met several more times at Sears, adding that he told her of his financial problems and she felt sorry for him. Then one Friday, according to Radford, "She took me by the hand and she took a deep breath and said, 'I want you to kidnap me.'"

Tane chuckled at the picture Radford was painting, as did several people around her, and she looked toward the jurors. None of them smiled, not even the sweet country man. Did they believe him?

"How did you react to that?" Chandler asked.

"Well, I was startled, you know," Radford said. "That was the fartherest thing from my mind. I didn't have any idea that's what she planned. Then, again, she said, 'Yeah.' Said, 'I want you to kidnap me.'"

Tane looked over her shoulder to see who was in the courtroom, who was hearing this story, who might believe it. There was the TV camera and the newspaper reporter. Soon the whole world would hear the lies. Radford continued and Tane turned back to face him. He never looked back at her.

"She just tried to convince me to do it," he said, looking at the jury and speaking softly. "She's got a way about her, she can be just as sweet as pie."

Tane's friends behind her giggled with that, but Tane did not. She looked at the jurors again, hoping to see a smile or a look of disbelief, but they gave her nothing.

"She said she didn't want her father's money, said that she didn't need it, she didn't want it. She wanted us to, or me, to buy a home in south Hall County with a pool. She likes water."

"Why did she want you to buy a home?" Chandler asked.

"So we could be together."

"Why did she want to have a pool?"

"She just loves to swim. She likes the water."

The guy is totally crazy, Tane thought. Did he really believe she would move in with him? Still, the jurors' faces didn't change.

Then Radford laid out the kidnapping plan, which he attributed to Tane, and explained how he picked her up at her house, switched cars at Burger King, and drove her to the trailer near Dahlonega. In his version she called him Don and he called her Honey. While they were in the trailer they "started to enjoy each other, but that didn't last but a couple of minutes. She just turned away and said she couldn't do anything, that she was too nervous."

The next morning, as he tied her up, "She started rubbing my back and told me she was sorry that she was so cold last night and that I had slept on the floor, and I told her that was all right, that we would be together in our new home."

The reason for tying her up in the first place, he said, was, "For a story. It was something that she could say when she got back home."

He said he didn't want to hurt Tane. "We was partners. We was friends. We was lovers."

Nobody laughed at Radford's story anymore. Not one juror had cracked the first smile. Tane's initial anger had turned to melancholy as Radford piled on twisted details that painted her as a woman who would desert her husband and children for this sick, desperate man. She was more helpless than when she was tied up in the trailer. She couldn't fight back. She could only sit and listen and hope that Lee Darragh could turn Radford's story against him.

That's what Darragh said he had in mind. He would use Radford's own words, plus the physical evidence, to show that Radford was "a loser" and that Tane was in a "very, very frightening situation."

In his closing argument, Darragh would tell the jury, "Donnie Ray Radford has apparently been watching Tane Shannon for fifteen years, from the time she was fourteen years old, a child, a freshman in high school, working at Dunaway Drugs during the Christmas season. Donnie Ray Radford has been watching Tane Shannon and watching and watching and watching, hoping for an opportunity to be with her, an unfulfilled fantasy on his part until August 10, 1992, and only then when he came to her home and took her at gunpoint under cover of a mask with holes in it."

He set up that argument with his cross-examination, during which Radford continued to claim he and Tane were partners in an attempt to extort half a million dollars from her father. He was less clear on the details, however, such as when he set out notes for Mike to find. Darragh picked and picked at those details before digging into Radford's money problems.

"Isn't it a fact," Darragh said, "that you had a fantasy that you were going to run off with Tane Shannon and have five hundred thousand dollars to boot because you didn't have any money to speak of, really. You lived with your parents, you made seven-fifty an hour but you wanted to be rich?"

"I did want to be with Tane, yes," Radford said, "and the money would be nice, it would. I can't say that it wouldn't."

In his attempt to paint Radford before the jury as a total loser, Darragh asked, "How much money were you going to get from the attempted bank robbery of First National Bank in 1987?"

Chandler immediately leapt to his feet with his objection. "I believe that's a completely improper question and I don't think the prosecution can go into that at all."

For several minutes the lawyers discussed the point with the judge, who would eventually agree with Chandler. The law would not allow questions about a crime Radford had committed previously. A copy of Radford's indictment and conviction would be included in the stack of material given to the jury for their deliberation, but no other mention of it could be made.

Darragh took another tack, with questions aimed at tripping up Radford on the details of his claimed relationship with Tane when she was a teenager. He wrapped up his cross-examination by asking Radford about the morning he left Tane tied up in the trailer to go make his ransom call. As he recalled his steps, Radford's testimony made clear for Tane the divine help she received during her escape. His delays in making his ransom call gave her time to free herself from the ropes and tape.

She hadn't been at Bonnell's house for more than a few

minutes with the deputy sheriffs when Radford returned. He was on his way back when she crossed the road and ran to the Davises' front door. How easy it would have been for him to catch her, to keep her from escaping, if nothing had slowed him — if the suspicious van or his own anxieties hadn't delayed him.

Tane wanted to spell it out for the jury, the judge, the lawyers, the world. The miracle was so obvious. All of the miracles were so obvious.

First, her children were sleeping when Radford burst into the house, so they didn't have to experience the horror of seeing their mother taken away at gunpoint.

Then, the kidnapper let her use the phone, and her father answered on the first ring at the office. He never did that. If he hadn't, Kaylan and Mick might have been left alone for hours.

Next, Alecia dropped by the house right after Radford took Tane away. She was able to look after the children until help came.

Then there was the Christian radio station and the preacher who reminded her that even the most wretched can be saved. Before she heard those words she had felt too guilty to pray. Why would God listen to her, she thought, on her deathbed? But the preacher on the radio said He would listen, so she did pray.

The vision of herself in the clouds while Mike and the kids played in the park — the feeling that she had been lifted high above the earth — was God's answer to her prayer, giving her encouragement and hope. She now knew that the sounds of wings in the trailer were angels with her, and the warmth she experienced were their arms around her.

Now she was learning of yet another miracle. Radford's delays and his drive through town before calling Mike with his ransom demand gave her enough time to escape and run to Bonnell's house, with her angels on the walls and the mantel and the tables, where she waited until the police arrested the kidnapper right outside.

Tane watched the jurors leave the courtroom to deliberate. They wouldn't see the miracles as clearly as she could, but she remained confident that they would return quickly with a guilty verdict.

✝ ✝ ✝

Billy Watson fell in line with the other jurors filing from their box in the courtroom into an adjacent room. The blinds on the tall window were open so he could look down from the second story to the rooftops around the Gainesville town square, which was quiet in the early afternoon. He expected to be out and back at home in time for supper. The evidence, in his mind, clearly showed Radford was guilty. He learned quickly that two of the women jurors felt otherwise.

When one of them said right off that Tane was "a spoiled rich girl," several others agreed. They based their conclusions on Tane's nice clothes, the Corvette she had driven as a teenager and her demeanor in court.

"She just didn't take it seriously enough," one of the women said, referring to Tane's occasional chuckles during Radford's testimony.

"Yeah," another added. "And this guy's too dumb to do something like this alone. He didn't even attempt to hide his trail."

"And where was the gun?" the first woman asked. "They never found the gun."

Steve Dunn, the restaurant manager Billy had gotten to know through the week, stood to emphasize his point, then said slowly, "The man is guilty beyond a shadow of a doubt." He argued that it was preposterous for Tane to be involved — that Radford obviously had made up the story while he was in jail awaiting his trial.

Billy had an ally. He hoped Steve could lead the other jurors to his conclusion.

✝ ✝ ✝

The day wore on toward night and the judge brought everybody back into the courtroom to tell the jury to take a dinner break.

"I don't know what's taking them so long?" Tane said softly to Mike. They were walking down the wide courthouse corridor and she didn't want to speak loudly enough for the surrounding reporters to hear her. "Do you think they believe him?"

Mike shrugged, avoiding any chance of being caught off guard. The newspaper and television and radio stations already had made celebrities of the Shannons. On page one of The Gainesville Times the previous afternoon, a huge color photograph of Mike showed him on the witness stand looking down as the tape recorder sat in front him playing the kidnapper's ransom demands. Mike had tried to laugh about it, joking that they didn't have to show so much of his nearly bald head. But they had captured one of the worst moments of his life.

Beside the picture in giant black letters were the words, "TANE: I DIDN'T PLOT MY OWN KIDNAPPING."

"Who's on trial here?" Tane had asked when she opened the paper at her own front door. "Can you believe this?"

Underneath the headline was a box highlighted in red telling readers, "Because of the interest in the Tane Shannon kidnapping case, The Times will have a hot line available each day beginning around 7 p.m." The notice then gave instructions for readers listen to updated information.

On the sidewalk in front of the courthouse, Mike and Tane discussed where they would eat supper. The judge had told the jury to come back and continue their deliberations, so the Shannons didn't want to be gone long. As they neared the corner at the square, Tane saw the afternoon paper in the box. In the spot where Mike's photo had appeared the day before was an equally large picture of Radford, his hand on his chin as if considering his next response.

This time the headline read, "RADFORD: WE WERE 'PARTNERS.'" A smaller headline below added, "DEFENDANT IN KIDNAPPING TRIAL CLAIMS TANE SHANNON ASKED TO BE ABDUCTED."

✝ ✝ ✝

In fact, when they broke for supper the jury was far from declaring Radford guilty. Two women were holding out, primarily because the prosecutor never produced a gun. They were also concerned about Mike's absence in the courtroom. Why wouldn't Tane's husband sit with her and support her through the ordeal of the trial? No one had told them that Mike was prohibited from staying in the courtroom because he was a witness in the case.

Billy Watson listened to the arguments but didn't join in, even though he was certain of Radford's guilt. He didn't think anybody would listen to a country man like him. As the deliberations dragged on, always focused on the little issues like Tane's clothes or whether she behaved appropriately in court, he began to clinch and relax his fists. They were going to let a guilty man go, and he couldn't let that happen. At some point he would have to step in.

When one of the women said, "I just can't be sure enough to vote guilty if they didn't find a gun," he slammed his clinched fist on the table.

"Look, we're wasting our time here talking about these little side issues," he said. "The man is guilty and we all know it. He could have thrown the gun anywhere."

As he spoke Billy got that feeling he had every morning when he was out in traffic, raising his hands and stopping the cars for the children to cross the street safely. Only now he was preventing further harm to a young woman and her family from a kidnapper.

When they came back from supper, the jury took another vote and found Radford guilty of kidnapping.

✝ ✝ ✝

Mike finally was allowed to sit beside Tane when the jury returned with its verdict. When they heard the word "guilty," they stayed in their seats, obeying the judge's admonition against emotional displays, and hugged each other across the chair arm that separated them. Before sentencing Radford, the judge asked if anyone wished to speak. Tane looked at Mike. Still angry about the grilling she received from the defense attorney, she was afraid to say anything. Her temper might control her.

"Do you want to say something?" she asked Mike.

Mike usually was terrible speaking in front of crowds, but he had to say something.

"From here or up there?" he asked.

"That will be fine, if you will stand," the judge said.

Mike stood and said, "It's with great respect I address the court today. I would like to say something before the court sentences that man. I sat here and took it the day she was kidnapped, the day she was taken from me and our children sleeping in our house. He came into this courtroom and he said awful things about my wife and I sat here and I took it and I have taken it up to here. We are victims of a terrible crime, the depth of which I did not know until I got in this courtroom. I didn't know he had a fixation or obsession on her since she was fourteen or fifteen years old. I did not know the depth of danger my wife was in. Only by the grace of God and her own sheer courage did she escape to be here today."

What Mike wanted to do was look Donnie Ray Radford in the eye and say to him and everybody else, "Not only did you kidnap my wife, you came in here and verbally raped her in front of the entire community, and prison is too good for you."

He controlled his temper, however, saying, "He has all of these rights. She is a victim and it seems like we've had no rights through this. I appreciate the court's time."

"Very well," the judge said as Mike sat.

Then the judge asked Radford to stand.

"Having been found guilty of count one of the indictment, kidnapping for ransom, Mr. Radford, the court hereby sentences you to prison for life."

Epilogue

Therefore, if anyone is in Christ, he is a new creation; the old has gone, the new has come!
– 2 Corinthians 5:17

By Tane Shannon
December 1997

When we began working on this book, Dick Parker asked me what I hoped it would accomplish. The answer came easily. I hope readers will commit their lives to Christ before they come face-to-face with death. I also want them to see the miracles God performed both to save my life here on earth and my eternal life. This book, the telling of my story, is my response to those miracles and to the blessings He continues to bestow upon me and my family.

Until a kidnapper took me from my family, I had lived my life like most people — like most Christians, dare I say. I avoided the "major" sins, remained true to my husband and children, and went to church on many Sundays. Yet, something was missing, and it affected every aspect of my life.

Mike and I were drifting apart in our marriage. He worked late most nights and I was so wrapped up in our children, I didn't miss him. Second only to the children — some would say it came first — was my devotion to developing my body through aerobics and weight training. My obsession was so strong that if I didn't complete my workout in two hours — the time limit for the gym's free nursery — I dropped off Kaylan and Mick at my mother's house then went back to the weight room and finished.

The results were clear. I loved the way I looked. Until, that is, at the point of a gun I saw my true self.

What followed was God's greatest miracle for me. He saved me. He gave me another opportunity. A new life. He allowed me to live out the words of Paul: "Therefore, if any-

191

one is in Christ, he is a new creation; the old has passed away, behold, the new has come."

From the moment He allowed me to live, I knew I must become a new creature. Nothing before or since has scared me more than that realization. How, after twenty-nine years of lukewarm response to Him, could I live a life worthy of Christ's salvation? And assuming I succeeded, what if the people I loved, particularly Mike, didn't like this "new creation"? After all, the woman he married wasn't on fire for Christ. She was a party girl who loved to laugh and play.

I decided not to tell anyone that I was changing. This would be just between me and God. I read my Bible secretly before Mike or the kids woke up each morning, and I prayed during that time for God to strengthen me to do good throughout the day. I also prayed that He would direct Mike toward the same spiritual path I had found. Like me, Mike had grown up in a Christian home and was committed to creating a similar environment for our children. But his fire for Christ was little more than an ember smoldering somewhere among the ashes.

Some of our most difficult times as a couple occurred during the first year following my kidnapping. I tried to focus on the positives. I escaped. The kids weren't harmed. They caught the kidnapper. Mike, on the other hand, questioned why God had allowed me to be taken. Why would He put our family through such a trial? I unfairly expected Mike to be as positive about the experience as I was. Yet, I hadn't told him of God's hand in it. I was afraid to — afraid he wouldn't believe me.

I had to ease him into the idea. Day by day I was more bold in the clues I left: an open Bible left on the table, a car radio tuned to a Christian station. Finally, when Mike saw me reading a book on angels one night, he asked. And, after months of prayer and Bible reading, I was ready.

"You've been telling everybody how strong I am," I said,

"but I'm not. I was a wimp that night, just waiting for Radford to kill me. It wasn't until I felt God's presence — and now I know it was angels in the room with me — that I knew I would be all right."

In Mike's eyes I saw the look I had feared. As hard as he tried, he couldn't mask his disbelief. Still, I was confident that he, too, eventually would believe.

"Something touched me deep inside that night," I continued. "It made me feel warm and calm. I didn't understand it then, but I do now."

We talked deep into the night about the coincidences I knew to be miracles and about the vision God gave me of Mike and the kids playing while I watched from the clouds. When we finally went to bed, he still wasn't totally convinced, but he knew I believed, and he believed in me. I could not have expected more.

That was four years ago. Today I would like to say we have found all the answers, we have achieved complete spiritual enlightenment and we are totally at peace with God. We are not. But, then, who is? I can say that we are searching together. God answered my most fervent prayer by touching Mike in a special way that has joined us in our spiritual walk. He has also given me the confidence to speak out for Him, even before large groups of people.

As I grow, I continue to deal with my anger at Donnie Ray Radford. The lies that were told at his trial still hurt deeply — not so much because they were told, rather, because some people who did not know the whole story believed them.

Dr. John Lee Taylor, our minister at the time of my kidnapping, helped me move from anger toward forgiveness. Anger against evil is justifiable, he said, and it is unhealthy to layer my own guilt on top of it. He encouraged me to focus on my anger as a first step toward forgiveness. At that point I wasn't even sure I wanted to forgive. But to forgive this man who has not sought my forgiveness is critical to my well-being. For if I cannot forgive Donnie Ray Radford, if I nurse my anger day by day, he will haunt me forever. I will never put him behind us.

My forgiveness, Dr. Taylor explained, does not need to imply that I would like to see Radford released from prison, for he has proven himself to be a danger to society and to my family in particular.

I have found immeasurable peace in the knowledge that God has used the kidnapping, and even the trial, for good. At the trial my cross-examination pushed me to publicly claim the miracles God gave us. That declaration emboldened me to tell the rest of my story to anyone who would listen.

Our lives continue to unfold according to God's plan. Our daughter Ryleigh was born in November 1995. Kaylan stood before our church and claimed Jesus Christ as her savior. And Mick demonstrates daily a true love for and growing understanding of the Lord.

More than ever, we look forward to tomorrow.

The Cover

"To God," painted by P.O. Vickery in 1888, hangs in Bonnell Davis' living room. She found the print, her favorite among her more than fifty angel paintings and figurines, years ago in the attic of the Davis homestead.